Also by Terry Barkley

The Gentle Scholar: The Forgotten Story of John M. Webb and the Webb School in Bell Buckle, Tennessee

One Who Served: Brethren Elder Charles Nesselrodt of Shenandoah County, Virginia

EVE'S WAIL

EVE'S WAIL

An Enslaved Woman Burned at the Stake in Colonial Virginia

TERRY BARKLEY

BRAYBREE
Publishing

Copyright © 2017 Terry Barkley
All rights reserved

Published by BrayBree Publishing Company LLC
FIRST EDITION

No part of this book may be reproduced, stored in or introduced into a retrieval system or transmitted in any form or by any means (electronic, mechanical, photocopying, recording, or otherwise) without the prior written permission of the publisher and copyright owner.

The scanning, uploading, and distribution of this book on the Internet or through any other means is not permitted without permission from the publisher and copyright owner.

ISBN-13: 978-1-940127-15-6

Printed in the United States of America

BrayBree Publishing Company LLC
P.O. Box 1204
Dickson, Tennessee 37056-1204

Visit our website at www.braybreepublishing.com

Front cover images: istockphoto.com
Back cover images: istockphoto.com, Patricia J. Hurst & Orange County Historical Society

*For my loving family,
my ninety-six year-old father, MAJ Hillard R. Barkley Sr., USA (Ret.),
and my sister, Betty Jean Barkley-Fawley,
our father's primary caregiver.
Always know that you are loved
and thank you sincerely for everything.*

ACKNOWLEDGEMENTS

First and foremost, I would like to thank Jim and Carolyn Miller of "Greenstone Farm LLC" for allowing me access to their property and for being both helpful and encouraging throughout the process of researching and writing this book. More than a decade ago, I showed up unannounced at Mount Airy (now Greenstone Farm), scene of Eve's burning, and introduced myself and my purpose for being there to Jim Miller. He and his family were then still living in the old Waugh farmhouse near the crest of the long winding hill. While Jim was aware that someone had been burned on the property in Colonial times, he knew little more than that. However, he smiled and said, "Let me show you something," whereupon we got into his truck and drove across the fields to a massive rock formation that I later learned was "Haystack Rock." It was summer and foliage nearly engulfed the rock formation, but we climbed over the rocks into the impressive site. The place really affected me, but it's hard to say why? There was a strange and eerie feeling about the place, something otherworldly, if you will. I just knew that this must have been the site where Eve was burned!

Leaving both my staff position at Bridgewater College and Virginia in 2005, I filed away the story of "Eve's Wail" for future reference. Some ten years later, I finally returned to live again in the Shenandoah Valley of Virginia, to Lexington, this time retired and on Medicare! I had already decided that in my retirement I would do historical research, write, and publish about the things that personally interested me. My last book, *The Gentle Scholar* (BrayBree Publishing), was published in 2015, the year I returned to Virginia. I also decided that *Eve's Wail: An Enslaved Woman Burned At the Stake in Colonial Virginia* would be the first project I would tackle in Virginia.

A special "thank you" goes out to my great friend and former colleague Nicholas P. Picerno of Bridgewater, Virginia, for writing the foreword to this book. Chief of Police and Campus Safety at Bridgewater College, Nick is also heavily involved in Civil War preservation and has served faithfully on a number of Civil War-related boards. He is Chairman Emeritus of the important Shenandoah Valley Battlefields Foundation.

The staff at the Orange County Historical Society in Orange, Virginia, have been wonderful and extremely helpful throughout this process. Jayne E. Blair, Jean McGann, and research historian Ann L. Miller deserve special recognition for their expert assistance and overall encouragement. Bethany Sullivan and Elka Alikhan at the James Madison Museum of Orange County History were also helpful. The Orange County Historical Society is located directly across Caroline Street in Orange from the James Madison Museum which, in turn, sits right beside historic St. Thomas's Episcopal Church. I thank Karin Merrill for the impromptu tour of the interior of St. Thomas's.

Leslie McGowan, deputy clerk at the Orange County Circuit Court, supplied me with a photocopy of the official record of Eve's trial and sentencing from the Orange County Record Books. This author donated a photocopy to the Orange County Historical Society.

Much of the research and most of the actual writing of this book took place in Lexington at the Preston Library at Virginia Military Institute and in the Leyburn Library and in the separate Law Library at Washington and Lee University. The staff of Special Collections and Archives at W & L have been most helpful and I wish to personally thank Tom Camden, Byron Faidley, Seth McCormick-Goodhart, and Lisa McCown for their efforts on my behalf. Alston Cobourn of the Leyburn Library staff cleared up a copyright issue for me, and staff member Elizabeth Anne Teaff helped me with the Virginia Topographical Maps. In Preston Library at VMI, Don Samdahl, Janet Holly, Accacia Mullen, Alicia Wheeler, and Ellen MacInnis were most helpful.

Troy Valos at the Norfolk (Virginia) Public Library (Sargeant Memorial Collection) went the extra mile in providing data concerning Peter Montague and his family, and I thank him sincerely for his professionalism.

I thank Dr. Clarence Geier of Harrisonburg, Virginia, and Dr. Matt Reeves at "Montpelier" near Orange, Virginia, for examining images of Haystack Rock taken by Jim Miller. Both gentlemen are professional archaeologists who have special interests in Civil War archaeology. Stanley S. Johnson of Charlottesville, a Consulting Geologist and brother of Orange County historian Patricia J. Hurst, also viewed and commented on the images and enlightened this author about greenstone, the rock most found on the old Mount Airy property now known as Greenstone Farm. Stan also examined and commented on the snapshots his sister took in 1986 of the supposed site of Eve's burning.

My old friend and colleague Dr. Jeff Bach of the Young Center at Elizabethtown College in Pennsylvania, has a running interest in this book from the application of English law to crime and punishment in Colonial America, to the early histories of Orange and Culpeper Counties in Virginia. His Bach ancestors settled in the area right after they arrived in 1738, being on the very tail end of the Germanna immigrations that started in 1714.

The Reverends David Butt and John Fogle were most helpful regarding my search for the site of "Eve's Wail." David was the pastor of the former Raccoon Ford Christian Fellowship near the burning site, and Pastor John Fogle shepherds the present Riverside Church in the same facility today.

Telephone interviews were conducted with Jim Miller, Patricia J. Hurst, Stanley S. Johnson (Pat's brother), Ann L. Miller, Frank S. Walker, Jr., David Butt, Sara Waugh Hurst, Alec Waugh, Wells Waugh, Sarah Waugh, Walker Summerville, and musician Billy Cooper (who, as a young military policeman, guarded the "Selma to Montgomery March" in 1965 in Alabama, this author's home state).

One of the most enjoyable experiences that I encountered in researching and writing this book was developing a friendship with Patricia J. Hurst of Rapidan, Virginia. An outstanding Orange County historian, her book on the history and people of Clark Mountain was my first introduction to the story of Eve's burning. At age eighty-three, Pat is sharp as a tack and is currently in the process of producing yet another book about her beloved Rapidan River and Orange County, the locale of the trial, sentencing, and execution of the slave woman Eve in 1745–1746.

I am grateful to Chris Williams and Andy Wolfe of Lexington, Virginia, for their assistance and encouragement in writing this book.

Finally, on a personal note, I must thank my sister, B.J. (Betty Barkley-Fawley), our ninety-six year-old father's primary caregiver in Huntsville, Alabama, for allowing me the time and space to pursue my historical and literary interests. Please always know that I love you guys dearly.

Terry Barkley
Deavers Alley
Lexington, Virginia
May 1, 2016

CONTENTS

Foreword *by Nicholas P. Picerno* ix
Preface *xi*
Prologue *xiii*

1. Eve *3*
2. Peter Mountague (Montague) *6*
3. Crime and Punishment on the Virginia Frontier *11*
4. Setting the Stage *18*
5. The Case of Rex v. Eve *26*
6. Mount Airy and the Waugh Family *32*
7. The Site of "Eve's Wail" *45*
Epilogue *57*

Appendix *61*
Bibliography *65*
Index *73*

FOREWORD

In 1746, in Orange County, Virginia, a slave with the name of Eve was convicted of killing her master by poisoning him and was ordered to be executed. The form of execution was heinous and, in a later time, would surely be considered cruel and unusual punishment. Her story would be forgotten with the passage of time and legend occupied the gaps created by time's passing. A well-researched history was needed to transform Eve's story into a historical narrative.

Terry Barkley has a penchant for critical research. I met Terry about fourteen years ago when he was employed as the Bridgewater College archivist and curator of special collections. Terry hailed from Alabama, and I recently moved from New Hampshire to become the Chief of Police at Bridgewater College. We both possessed great affection for American Civil War history and eventually this mutual interest led us to meet. We would discuss the "War" from our individual perspectives, North and South, while never taking sides. We travelled to battlefields where I listened to Terry's interpretation of the tactics employed on those deadly grounds.

I soon recognized Terry's extraordinary abilities as a research historian. Not content with established history, Terry wished to pursue sources and verify that whatever had been accepted as fact truly was factual. As a Harvard-trained archivist and museum curator, Terry has a special reverence for archives and special collections. During his travels he tenaciously researches his subject and attempts to uncover the obscure and illustrate its relevance.

In telling the story of Eve's trial and punishment, Terry Barkley's ability to transform oral tradition into history becomes most evident. His research is akin to the most ardent criminal investigator who wishes to seek closure on a cold case. He has woven Eve's story into a wonderfully researched narrative relating a little known sordid facet of Virginia's history. It is a compelling account and it also reveals Terry's odyssey to research the story and find the location of "Eve's Wail" to ensure she is silent no longer.

Nicholas P. Picerno
Chairman Emeritus
Shenandoah Valley Battlefields Foundation

PREFACE

This little book centers on a single tragic incident in the history and legal history of Colonial Virginia, the burning of an African-American woman named Eve in Orange County in 1746. While many will be surprised that someone was actually burned at the stake in America like Joan of Arc in France, the fact that this was a court ordered execution prescribed by English law, then the laws of the English colonies in America, makes it all the more intriguing. As the reader will learn, Eve's burning was simply one of many such court ordered burnings in the American colonies.

Rex as in Rex v. Eve is Latin for king. The phrase is used to designate the king as the party prosecuting an accused in a criminal case. Oyer and Terminer is French for "to hear and decide." It is the name of a state court authorized to hear and determine all treasons, felonies, and misdemeanors. In Colonial times, this court was normally empowered to prescribe appropriate punishment for offenders, punishment based primarily on English Common Law, the laws of both England and the American colonies. For further clarification and definition, please refer to John Bouvier, *A Law Dictionary, Adapted to the Constitution and Laws of the United States*... (Philadelphia, PA: Childs and Peterson, 1856).

The conversion of the Julian calendar (Old Style) to the Gregorian calendar (New Style), that established January 1st as the start of the yearly calendar, was not adopted by Great Britain until 1752. The Julian calendar in England started March 25th, with the Gregorian calendar in England beginning January 1st. Thus, one must convert the day and the month. The Julian or Old Style calendar was used in documents in England and the American colonies before 1752. Years are often written as 1745/46, for example, which is called double or dual dating. To avoid confusion, for the purposes of this study the Gregorian or New Style calendar will be employed with January 1st being the first day of the year. Thus, Peter Montague was allegedly poisoned by Eve and died in 1745, and Eve was tried and convicted of his murder and executed in 1746.

PROLOGUE

On Thursday, January 23, 1746, a female African American slave named Eve was charged with "petit" or petty treason. She was duly tried and convicted of fatally poisoning her master, Peter Montague, in Orange County, Virginia. On Wednesday, January 29, she was burned at the stake on a knoll near the first county courthouse. The site of her burning became known as "Eve's Wail."

In 1986, R. Monroe Waugh, the man who named "Eve's Wail" and also owned the site, showed two prominent Orange County historians, both female, where Eve was burned. To this day, both women remember the eerie and foreboding feeling that came over them when viewing the site, something almost supernatural.

EVE'S WAIL

1

EVE

Very little is known about Eve. She was owned by Peter Montague and judged to be worth fifty pounds. In comparison, another slave named Peter, who was hanged for murder and beheaded in Orange County in 1737, was judged to be worth thirty-seven pounds and ten shillings. A male and female slave also belonging to Montague and included in his estate were judged to be worth thirty-five and twenty pounds, respectively.

Eve may have been a house slave and servant who was entrusted to handle food and drink for her master and his family. In an area where qualified physicians were quite scarce or even non-existent, trusted slaves were allowed to administer natural medicinal "cures" to whites and slaves alike. She may very well have held this position and been allowed to administer "African medicine." If so, this elevated status among the other slaves would signify her importance to the overall well-being of her white master and his family and justify her increased monetary worth of fifty pounds.[1]

Among the "diverse witnesses" who testified against Eve at her trial was one who came from a long distance. Hugh Noden, Gentleman, "a witness for our Sovereign Lord, the King," traveled fifty miles from Caroline County to testify against Eve. Was he merely a representative of the Crown or did he actually know Eve personally? Could he have been Eve's former owner and master in Caroline County? Finally, might Eve have been an Igbo African like some of the slaves at Orange County's "Montpelier?" The Igbo were an ethnic group from southern Nigeria who were targeted by slave traders.[2]

How was Eve personally treated by her master and his family? Was she abused—abuse in addition to the already subjugated horrors of slavery? Did that treatment include abuse physically, mentally, or even sexually? What was Eve's relationship with Anthorit, Mrs. Peter Montague, and with the children, Sarah and Elizabeth?

Why did Eve wait until the Montagues moved from Spotsylvania County to Orange County to poison or "conjure" her master? Was she being torn from family and friends among the slaves in Spotsylvania County—her support group, if you will—and forced to abide in a new and strange place?

We know that when Peter Montague's estate was adjudicated in 1746, with his wife as the administrator, his human possessions included "one negro man" and "one negro girl."[3] Were they related to Eve by blood or otherwise? What was Eve's relationship with them? Were they a family?

---

1. Orange County Order Book 4, 455. Orange County Order Book 1, 180–181. Orange County Will Book 3, 89. Ruth Trickey and Sam Sparacio, compilers and editors, *Pamunkey Neighbors of Orange County, Virginia*. Baltimore, MD: Gateway Press, Inc., 1985, 47–48. Patricia J. Hurst, *The History and People of Clark Mountain, Orange County, Virginia*. Rapidan, VA: P. J. Hurst, 1989, 133–134. Ann L. Miller, *The Short Life and Strange Death of Ambrose Madison*. Orange, VA: Orange County Historical Society, 2001, 67, 70–72.

2. Orange County Order Book 4, 454–455. See Douglas B. Chambers, *Murder at Montpelier: Igbo Africans in Virginia*. Jackson, MS: University Press of Mississippi, 2005.

3. Orange County Will Book 3, 89. Sparacio, 47–48.

There are enough open questions about Eve—and her burning—to fill the pages of a good novel or even a screen play. The canvas is nearly clean and beckons only for the imagination to paint the story.

Coat of Arms of the Mountague (Montague) Family in Virginia
(History and Geneaology of Peter Montague of Nansemond and Lancaster Counties, Virginia, and His Descendants, 1621–1894)

2

PETER MOUNTAGUE (MONTAGUE)

The Mountague (Montague) surname is believed to be Norman in origin and translates as being "of or from a sharp or pointed mountain"—a mountain peak. The Mountagues include English, Irish, Italian, and French antecedents.[1] The family lineage in America can be traced to the early 1600s to Peter, second son of Peter Mountague of Boveny, parish of Burnham, Buckinghamshire, England. Peter and his wife, Ellenor Allen, sailed for America and the colony of Virginia on the *Charles* in 1621.[2]

---

1. Generally speaking, before about 1700, the name was normally spelled Mountague; afterwards, usually Montague, though the former spelling persists in the case of *Rex v. Eve*. George William Montague, *History and Genealogy of Peter Montague, of Nansemond and Lancaster Counties, Virginia, and his Descendants, 1621–1894*. Amherst, MA: Press of Carpenter & Morehouse, 1894, 449. Hereafter, the title is listed as *HGPM*.

2. Montague, *HGPM*, 39, 49, 449. Annie Lash Jester and Martha Woodroof Hiden, *Adventurers of Purse and Person: Virginia, 1607–1625*. 1st edition, Order of First Families of Virginia, 1607–1620, Princeton, NJ: Princeton University Press, 1956, 250.

Peter Montague (1718–1745), Eve's master, was only twenty-seven years old when he died. He was survived by his wife and two daughters. He had no sons. Born in Middlesex County, Virginia, on March 28, 1718, Peter was a fifth-generation Montague whose parents were Thomas Jr. (c. 1694–1756), and Grace Montague (died March, 1726).[3] The family were members of Christ Church Parish in Middlesex County, where Peter was baptized on April 27, 1718.[4] He married Anthorit (Antherit), possibly Ann Theriott [Theriet, Therritt, Therriatt], in 1738 before moving to Orange County. They had two daughters: Sarah, born January 29, 1739, and Elizabeth, born 1744 in either Spotsylvania or Orange County. Anthorit herself was born in 1718 at St. Mary's, Essex County, Virginia. She and Peter were both about twenty years old when they married. Anthorit died between 1756–1757 at St. Thomas, Orange County, Virginia, age thirty-eight or thirty-nine.[5]

There are two scenarios as to when Peter moved his family to Orange County. The first claims that the Montagues moved there in 1739 when both Peter and Anthorit were about twenty-one years of age.[6] The other scenario speculates that Peter Montague and his family did not move to Orange County until the summer of 1745, coming from Spotsylvania County. In June 1745, Peter purchased two hundred eleven acres of land in Orange County near the former post office of Pine Top. A portion of his homestead was still standing in 1890. A granddaughter of Peter and Anthorit's daughter,

---

3. Montague, *HGPM*, 64–65, 70–71.

4. *Ibid*, 70–71. Montague, *HGPM* (2003 edition), 87–88. John Otto Yurechko,`*Christ Church Parish Register, Middlesex County, Virginia, 1553–1812*. Westminster, MD: Family Line Publications, 1996, 72.

5. Orange County Will Book 2, 236. Anthorit may be a misreading (or kludge) of Ann Theriott et al. At least one source lists her name as Elizabeth Ann Theriott. She may have been the daughter of Peter and Ann [–?–] Theriott or possibly the daughter of Elizabeth Therriatt, who was the daughter of William Therriatt of Lancaster County, Virginia, and the wife of Thomas Taylor (married 1706). Virginia M. Meyer and John Frederick Dorman, *Adventurers of Purse and Person, Virginia, 1607-1624/5*. 3rd edition, revised and edited, Order of First Families of Virginia, 1607-1624/5, Richmond, VA: The Dietz Press, Inc., 1987, 305. Montague, *HGPM* (2003), 88. John Frederick Dorman, *Adventurers of Purse and Person: Virginia 1607-1624/5*. 4th edition, Vol. 2, Baltimore, MD: Genealogical Publishing Company, 2004–2007, 2:664.

6. George William Montague, 64-65. Robert V. Montague, *HGPM* (2003), 87.

Sarah, Mrs. Dr. J. Minor Goodwin, then more than eighty years-old, lived in the house.[7] The Montagues lived in St. George Parish while in Spotsylvania County. This scenario seems more plausible as two sales of land in that county where made by Peter Montague—called Peter Montague Junior to distinguish him from his uncle Peter, his father's brother, who also settled in Orange County—the sales (indentures) being recorded in Spotsylvania County for August 6, 1744. One plot was for eighty-four acres and the other for ninety-eight acres. It is known that other Montague family members also lived in Spotsylvania County.[8]

If it is true that the Peter Montague family actually moved to Orange County during the summer of 1745, then events occurred in quick succession leading to Peter's demise. Eve allegedly poisoned her master on August 19, 1745, and he lingered in agony for four months until he expired on December 27, 1745.

> …Peter Montague did most grievously languish from the aforesaid nineteenth day of August in the…until the twenty-seventh day of December…Peter Montague so mortally poisoned died Eve falsely traiterously and feloniously of her malice forethought with the poison…did kill, poison, and murder… [9]

Where Peter was buried is not known, but it was possibly on his own property near Pine Top or at St. Thomas in Orange County.

Anthorit was the administrator of her husband's estate. She made an appraisement of his personal property, amounting to ninety-seven pounds, that was recorded in Orange County on July 24, 1746. Peter's personal property included two enslaved human beings, "one negro man" worth thirty-five pounds, and "one negro

---

7. Robert V. Montague, *HGPM* (2003), 87. Orange County Deed Book 10, 171,173. Miller, *Ambrose Madison*, 69.

8. Spotsylvania County Deed Book D, 128, 130. Sparacio, 42–43. On two occasions, once before her husband's death, October 1, 1745, and once after, August 5, 1746, Anthorit Montague traveled to Spotsylvania County to affirm in court that the deeds from both land sales were proper.

9. Orange County Order Book 4, 454–455. Robert V. Montague, *HGPM* (2003), 87. Sparacio, 46. Hurst, *Clark Mountain*, 132, 134.

girl" worth twenty pounds. Whether Eve was related by blood to either of them is not known.[10]

A division of Peter's personal property was recorded on October 28, 1756, whereby Reuben Daniel, who married the widow Anthorit before 1756, received the household goods and stock worth thirty-eight pounds, twelve shillings, and seven pence; John Stevens, who married Sarah, one of Peter and Anthorit's two daughters, received a man servant and bed valued at thirty pounds, nine shillings, and seven pence; and Elizabeth, the unmarried daughter, took a servant woman valued at thirty-six pounds, seven shillings, and four pence.[11]

The division of Peter Montague's real estate of two hundred eleven acres was recorded on October 25, 1759, whereby John Stevens "in the right of his wife" Sarah, received one hundred twenty and one half acres of land, and Elizabeth took ninety and one half acres of land including the "dwelling house, out houses and peach orchard." Sarah and Elizabeth were also mentioned in their grandfather's will, Thomas Montague Jr., who died in 1756.[12]

---

10. Orange County Order Book 4, May 22, 1746, 470. Orange County Order Book 5, July 24, 1746, 2. Orange County Will Book 3, 89. Sparacio, 47–48. Dorman, *Adventurers of Purse and Person*, 4th ed., 2:664.

11. Orange County Will Book 2, 236. Robert V. Montague, *HGPM* (2003), 87–88; Elizabeth later married James Daniel. She died at age eighty-three on January 17, 1826. Robert V. Montague, *HGPM* (2003), 87–88. Dorman, *Adventurers of Purse and Person*, 4th ed., 2:664.

12. George William Montague, 64–65, 70-71. Robert V. Montague, *HGPM* (2003), 87–88.

3

CRIME AND PUNISHMENT ON THE VIRGINIA FRONTIER

Common Law and the Acts of Parliament together comprised the civil law of England, the laws of which were extended to the English colonies in America.[1]

Punishments for certain crimes were specified by English law with high treason and "petit" or petty treason being the most "heinous." The penalty for high treason in England (with variations in the colonies) ordered that

> ...the offender should be dragged to the gallows, hanged, and cut down while still alive; that his entrails [disemboweling] should be taken out and burned, supposedly while he was still

---

1. George Lewis Chumbley, *Colonial Justice in Virginia: The Development of a Judicial System, Typical Laws and Cases of the Period*. Richmond, VA: The Dietz Press, 1938, 13.

living; and that he should be beheaded and quartered, and that his head and quarters should be "at the King's disposal."[2]

In eighteenth century Virginia, alleged slave attempts by secretive means of poisoning or "conjuring" whites and even other slaves produced sustained levels of white hysteria and revulsion, these attempts being met with prompt retaliation. At least 175 slaves, 143 men and 32 women in 22 Virginia counties, were accused of poisoning in court records and other legal documents up to about 1800, where "a large proportion had white masters or overseers as their ostensible targets." Even mere threats of poisoning by slaves were taken very seriously by whites. There was even fear that unscrupulous whites might use slaves to do their dirty work for them against their white enemies.[3]

While Orange County, Virginia, was not immune to slaves poisoning their white masters and overseers, outright or "ordinary" murder was also present. Ambrose Madison, who received the patent to the land now known as "Montpelier" in 1723, did not actually move with his family to the tract until 1732. Orange County author and historian Frank S. Walker Jr., writes that "It could be years, if ever, before a master might settle on the land which his slaves and servants had been clearing and farming." Hence, the importance and almost total power and control assumed by the overseer managing the property for his absentee employer.

Ambrose Madison's arrival at "Mount Pleasant" (later, "Montpelier") "triggered another facet of slavery which haunted the white population," and in mere months he was dead. Pompey, a slave from another plantation who was probably rented or on loan to Madison, was convicted of Madison's murder and was executed. The court placed a monetary value on Pompey as required by law since the Crown was taking a master's private property via

---

2. Arthur P. Scott, *Criminal Law in Colonial Virginia*. Chicago, IL: The University of Chicago Press, 1930, 161–162.

3. Philip D. Morgan, *Slave Counterpoint: Black Culture in the Eighteenth-Century Chesapeake & Low Country. Published for the Omohundro Institute of Early American History and Culture, Williamsburg, Virginia*. Chapel Hill, NC: The University of North Carolina Press, 1998, 612–613.

execution, and that sum was paid to the master. Two Madison slaves were convicted as accomplices in Ambrose Madison's murder and ordered punished and then returned to Madison's widow, Frances Taylor Madison. She apparently simply put them back to work, leading to speculation as to what life with Ambrose Madison had really been like![4]

On June 23, 1737, Peter, slave of John Riddle, was convicted of murdering his master with an ax and a knife.[5] Charged with "petit," or petty treason, he was sentenced to be hanged. The Sheriff cut off his head and stuck it on a pole outside the first Orange County Courthouse "to deter others from doing the Like."[6]

In her book about Clark Mountain and its people, Patricia Hurst includes an excerpt from the county records of Peter's trial, conviction, and execution:

> [On the] twenty eight day of May about two o'clock in the night…Peter…with one narrow ax of the value of two shillings (and one knife of the value of six pences) which the said Peter…then and there in his hands held upon the said John Riddle then his master in the peace of God being willfully and of his malice forethought did make an assault…with said ax and knife feloniously and trayterously upon his hands held upon his head with great force did strike and his throat did cut…that with the said blow, wound and cut throat the

---

4. Frank S. Walker Jr., *Remembering: A History of Orange County, Virginia*. Orange, VA: Orange County Historical Society, 2004, 183. See Miller, …*Ambrose Madison* (2001) and Chambers, *Murder at Montpelier* (2005).

5. Thomas Riddle, according to Arthur P. Scott in *Criminal Law in Colonial Virginia* (1930), 196. After murdering his master, Peter reportedly escaped on a stolen horse but was "captured, tried promptly, and sentenced to death." *Ibid*, 196.

6. Orange County Order Book 1, June 23, 1737, 180–181. Hurst, …*Clark Mountain*, 133–135. Miller, …*Ambrose Madison*, 67. William H. B. Thomas, "Law and Medicine in Colonial Orange County." *Bicentennial Series* #3 (July 1975). Orange County Bicentennial Commission. Orange, VA: Printed by Green Publishers, Inc., 8–9. Dr. A. G. Grinnan, "The Burning of Eve in Virginia," *The Virginia Magazine of History and Biography*, Vol. III, No. 3 (January 1896), 309. W. W. Scott, *A History of Orange County, Virginia*. Richmond, VA: Everett Waddey Co., 1907, 134. Ulysses P. Joyner Jr., *The First Settlers of Orange County, Virginia*. Baltimore, MD: Published for the Orange County Historical Society by Gateway Press, Inc., 1987, 145–146.

head and skull of the said John Riddle then his master then and there in two parts Did wound cut and break giving him a mortal blow and wound of which blow and wound the said John Riddle instantly then and there died and so the said Peter...willfully wickedly, feloniously and trayterously did slay kill and murder...

On the 23rd day of June 1737...Peter...being indicted for feloniously murthering his master...upon his arraignment pleaded guilty. [The court ordered that Peter] be hanged by the neck until he be dead and the court are of the opinion that the said Peter worth thirty seven pounds ten shillings curt money.[7]

Later, as they probably "soon tired of this ghastly spectacle," the "honorable justices" ordered the head moved a few miles away to the locality of the crime, a place which became known in Orange County as Negrohead Run (or Negro-head Run) and, later, as Negro Run.[8] However, W. W. Scott, in his *A History of Orange County, Virginia*, doubted that Negrohead Run was named for this inhumane incident. Also, this may or may not have been Peter, Scott claiming that the victim had been beheaded and "drawn and quartered," which was usually the case in England, but not so much in the American colonies. Finally, Scott stated that this was not verified in the county records and, if true, may have occurred before Orange County was created.[9]

While Eve's trial and burning was considered the most sensational and notorious of the slave trials in Orange County, such trials often took on a life of their own.

Letty, a slave on loan from Mrs. Harriet Potter of Middlesex County, was tried in Orange County in 1748 by a Court of Oyer and

---

7. Orange County Order Book 1, June 23, 1737, 180–181. Hurst, *Clark Mountain*, 133–134. In the 1500s, the English Parliament made the murdering of a master by a slave an act of treason punishable by death. Thus, executions for Peter and Eve's murderous crimes of "petit" or petty treason were so ordered. See Walker, *Remembering*, 183.

8. Grinnan, 309.

9. W. W. Scott, 133.

Terminer on suspicion of poisoning two people, one a white overseer and the other a slave. Richard Sims lingered in agony for five months before expiring, and Simon, a slave, suffered for six months before dying. At her trial on May 26, 1748, Letty was acquitted of the charges and released to her mistress. Dr. A. G. Grinnan of Madison County felt that Letty was acquitted because the court had "the feeling that the horrible scene so recently enacted at the burning of Eve should not be repeated in Orange county."[10]

Ann L. Miller, a Virginia state architectural historian and research historian for the Orange County Historical Society, notes in Appendix 5 of her *The Short Life and Strange Death of Ambrose Madison* (2001) that poisonings were usually done in a single dose and occurred in mid to late summer during the growing season. The poisonous substance may have been a natural or botanical extract or compound that grew and was most potent in warmer weather:

> The apparent single doses, along with the prolonged deaths, suggest that these cases involved doses of poison that were not sufficient to kill outright, but that involved a severe enough insult to the body to result in gradual failure of one or more major organs and eventual death.[11]

Miller believes that the small number of poisoning cases in Orange County (only four in the area from about 1720 to around 1750), "along with the diverse verdicts in the murder trials,"

> suggest that these were fair trials, even against an undercurrent of whites' ever-present fear of slave revolts and attacks… [and] argue against these trials being examples of panic or blind racism in response to death from poisonous or tainted foods or from an illness not related to poisoning. Certainly these were not 'show trials,' with execution a foregone conclusion.[12]

---

10. Orange County Order Book 5, May 26, 1748, 113. Miller, *Ambrose Madison*, 68. Walker, *Remembering*, 184. Grinnan, 310.

11. Miller, *Ambrose Madison*, 68-69.

12. Miller, *Ambrose Madison*, 70.

Even Eve was reportedly given a fair trial.

And, as with the case of Eve who may well have been allowed to administer medicines to her white master and his family, some slaves functioned as country doctors in areas of the Virginia frontier where there were few if any qualified physicians. Traditional medicines used by African healers and herbalists, including the use of botanical compounds as remedies, were the norm. These practices were supported by a similar European folk tradition. However, as the frequency of slave poisonings increased in Virginia, legislation via the 1748 Act (included as part of the statutes prescribing punishment for slaves guilty of murder) was enacted to severely limit slaves from acting as healers.[13]

Slaves would sometimes be granted "benefit of clergy" for a first offense, but the "privilege could only be once enjoyed." This plea stemmed from a time when ministers did most of the teaching to a mostly illiterate populace; thus, the need to preserve those who could read and write was paramount for the good of society. In 1767, however, Tom, slave of John Baylor, in Orange, broke into the home of Erasmus Taylor and took items judged to be worth about twenty-five cents (eighteen pence). Tom tried to plea "benefit of clergy," but he had already been granted such for a previous offense and he was executed.[14]

During Colonial times, the blacks living in Orange County were almost all slaves, though a few may have been free, they too "living difficult and uncertain lives." Slaves were deemed real property and had no personal rights. At one point, there was even a move to consider slaves real estate rather than personal property.[15]

---

13. William Waller Hening, *The Statutes at Large: Being a Collection of All the Laws of Virginia…Vol. VI*, Published For the Jamestown Foundation of the Commonwealth of Virginia. Charlottesville, VA: The University Press of Virginia, 1969, 105. Miller, *Ambrose Madison*, 70–71.

14. Grinnan, 309. W. W. Scott, 136. Thomas, "Law and Medicine in Colonial Orange County," 9–10. Walker, *Remembering*, 184. For additional incidents regarding crimes and punishments in Orange County during the Colonial period, see W. W. Scott, 133–137.

15. William H. B. Thomas, "Orange County Be It Remembered," *Bicentennial Series #1* (January 1975). Orange County Bicentennial Commission. Orange, VA: Printed by Green Publishers, Inc., 8. George Lewis Chumbley, *Colonial Justice in Virginia: The Development of a Judicial System, Typical Laws and Cases of the Period*. Richmond, VA: The Dietz Press, 1938, 73.

An enumeration and distribution of the population was done for Orange County in 1782, after the Revolution, though the results probably reflected pre-war days, as well. Of the total population of the county—6,258—nearly half were blacks. There were some 550 heads of families named. Of those, 60% of white households were listed as having blacks, presumably all slaves. Of those owning slaves, nearly all claimed owning less than fifty slaves, and 70% had less than ten slaves. The county's largest slave owner had 88 slaves, and only six others had 50 or more slaves. Most, like the Peter Montague family, had only a few slaves who either worked the land or were house servants. The Montague family claimed three slaves: a man, a women (Eve), and a girl.[16]

Concurrently, the Native American "problem" east of the Blue Ridge Mountains had largely subsided by the time Orange County was formed.

> ...Indians east of the mountains had almost entirely disappeared—ravaged by diseases for which they had no immunity, pushed back as the relentless surge of westward expansion began.[17]

---

16. Thomas, "Orange County Be It Remembered," 8. Orange County Will Book 3, 89. Sparacio, 47–48.

17. Thomas, "Orange County Be It Remembered," 8–9.

4

∾

SETTING THE STAGE

Eve's alleged crime, trial, conviction and sentencing, and prescribed execution occurred between August 19, 1745, and January 29, 1746, in Orange County, Virginia, the Old Dominion state.

Nestled in the central Piedmont region of the Commonwealth of Virginia some 28 miles northeast of Charlottesville, Orange County was formed from Spotsylvania County in 1734 and named for William III of England, Prince of Orange. Today, it is bounded by Culpeper, Madison, Greene, Albemarle, Louisa and Spotsylvania counties of Virginia.

By order of Lieutenant Governor Alexander Spotswood of the Virginia Colony, the first European settlement in what is now Orange County was established at Germanna in 1714 and 1717. It was an outpost against the Indians, the settlement then being on the western limits of the Virginia frontier. By 1725, however, the 1717 colony at Germanna had moved up the Rapidan River and its tributary, the Robinson, many settling permanently in what is now Madison County, created in 1792 from Orange County. Many of the German colonists eventually intermarried and many families trace their descent today to these stalwart Germans of the Piedmont region.[1]

Orange County was established in 1734 from portions of Spotsylvania County. While most county boundaries in the Virginia Colony stopped at the Blue Ridge Mountains, it claimed lands stretching all the way to the Mississippi River and the Great Lakes. Once thought to be the largest county ever created (a situation that lasted only four years), little of its western lands had been occupied by the English. Augusta County was created in 1738 and absorbed most of the western tract of Orange County. The expansive boundaries of both counties promoted further western expansion and served as a hedge against the French claim to the Ohio Valley.[2]

Writing in "The Burning of Eve in Virginia" in *The Virginia Magazine of History and Biography* (1896), Dr. A.G. Grinnan of Madison County claims that when Orange County was created in August, 1734, separated from Spotsylvania County which was created in 1721, the county's holdings included the present counties of Culpeper, Rappahannock, Greene, and Madison counties east of the Blue Ridge Mountains, most of the Valley of Virginia (Shenandoah Valley), and the country west of the Allegheny Mountains to the Ohio River Valley! Overseeing this "veritable principality" were the civil and military officials of the municipal Court of Orange County.[3]

---

1. The site of Germanna and Alexander Spotswood's "Enchanted Castle" ("Porto Bella") have reverted back to nature although foundation and formal garden remains can still be seen. James W. Green, *Orange Court House, 1861–1865*, Published by the Orange County Civil War Centennial Committee. Orange, VA: Printed by The Orange Review, 1965, 1–3. See also http://umwhisp.net/germanna/node/46. An old friend and former colleague of this author, Dr. Jeff Bach, Director of the Young Center at Elizabethtown College in Pennsylvania, has a special interest in the formation of Orange and Culpeper Counties: "That's where my Bach ancestors settled right after they arrived in 1738 (they were the very tail end of the Germanna immigrations that started in 1714). Email from Jeff Bach to author, February 1, 2016.

2. W.W. Scott, *A History of Orange County, Virginia*, 18, 21–22, 30.

3. Grinnan, 308.

The northern part of Orange County encompassed some of Alexander Spotswood's original land holdings of 85,000 acres which included lands on both sides of the Rapidan River, the present Culpeper County being on the northern banks with Orange County on the southern.

Today, U.S. Highway 522 (Zachary Taylor Highway) crosses the Rapidan not far from Somerville Ford (originally called "The Governor's Ford") separating Orange and Culpeper counties. Raccoon Ford and Morton's Ford are further down river (east) and all three fords were utilized historically including heavily during the Civil War. The Eighteenth-century Raccoon Ford and ferry site was further up river than the Nineteenth-century Raccoon Ford used during the Civil War. At the Eighteenth-century ford site, the Marquis de Lafayette's troops and General "Mad" Anthony Wayne and his Pennsylvania Brigade crossed within days of each other in 1781 before combining forces en route to Yorktown where the British were defeated and surrendered. South of the modern bridge on Route 522 crossing the Rapidan, Route 636 (River Road) turns west off the highway heading to Rapidan (Station). Route 611 (Raccoon Ford Road in Orange County), turns east off of U. S. Highway 522 and runs along the old Mount Airy property where Eve was burned. The banks and depth of the Rapidan River have changed considerably over time. The original River Road washed away in 1937, and terrible flooding has always plagued the river.[4]

Walker Somerville's family have owned lands along the Rapidan River since 1795, when James Somerville obtained lands along the banks of the river. The family built a mill at Somerville Ford which is a little up river from the U.S. Highway 522 bridge and at a bend in the river heading westward towards Rapidan (Station). Somerville Ford, like other fords on the river, is located right before some rapids where the water is usually shallower and the bottom sandy. When James Somerville died, his lands were divided among five sons. "Sumervillia," the home place of the Somerville

---

4. Patricia J. Hurst, *Soldiers, Stories, Sites, and Fights, Orange County, Virginia, 1861-1865, and the Aftermath*. Rapidan, VA: P. J. Hurst, 1998, 130-131.

family, is still standing but is now in other hands. According to Walker Somerville, the family lost the house and their fortune in the 1920s, and while probably land-rich, they are but "poor dirt farmers" today.[5]

Affording a panoramic view in all directions, Clark Mountain, formerly known as Chestnut Mountain, rising some 1,082 feet above sea level in Orange County, is the prominent feature of the northern part of the county along the Rapidan River. Clark Mountain includes the main mountain and two spurs or arms. It runs parallel to the Rapidan River for about three miles, the river being not only the boundary line today between Orange and Culpeper Counties, but essentially the boundary line between the Union (north of the Rapidan) and Confederate armies (south of the Rapidan) during the Civil War. The Confederate defensive line of breastworks running along the rolling hills south of the Rapidan comprised the "Rapidan Line," the river "effectively being the northern border of the Confederacy from March 1862 to May 1864."[6]

The Clark family settled on top of the mountain that bears their name. It is a part of the ridge-line of hills mainly south of the Rapidan known as the Southwest Mountains or Little Mountains, the Blue Ridge Mountains in the distance being called the Great Mountains. Clark Mountain served as a signal station for both the Confederate and Union armies and played a significant role in the Battle of Cedar Mountain fought nearby in Culpeper County on August 9, 1862.

Skirmishes were also fought on and around the mountain during the war. Today, a radio tower complex marks the site of the signal stations.[7]

---

5. Author's telephone conversation with Walker Somerville, January 13, 2016. John R. Maass provides evidence in *The Road to Yorktown: Jefferson, Lafayette and the British Invasion of Virginia* (Charleston, SC: The History Press, 2015), 108, 114, 169, that both Lafayette and Wayne crossed the Rapidan River at the eighteenth-century Raccoon Ford site, Lafayette followed later by Wayne.

6. Green, 22–23. https://en.wikipedia.org/wiki/Orange, Virginia.

7. Patricia J. Hurst, *The War Between the States, 1862-1865, Rapidan River Area of Clark Mountain, Orange County, Virginia*. Rapidan, VA: P. J. Hurst, 1989, v, vi.

The view from atop Mount Airy, now Greenstone Farm, where Eve was burned. It shows the Rapidan River basin with the Blue Ridge Mountains in the background. (Jim Miller)

Fortunately, Orange County was not occupied by either army during the Civil War for any extended length of time and the records at the present Orange County Courthouse in Orange, the county seat, are complete from the county's organization in 1734 to the present day. This is an amazing circumstance given that many records in other Virginia and Southern counties were either lost or destroyed.[8]

The first permanent courthouse for Orange County was built on Spotswood holdings south of the river near Somerville Ford. It was here that Eve was tried and convicted of poisoning her master, Peter Montague, and where she was sentenced to be burned. The site of her burning is on a knoll or hillock south of the courthouse on property later known as Mount Airy. From the crest of the hill at Mount Airy there is a beautiful and commanding view of the Rapidan River basin with the Blue Ridge Mountains beyond. The land south of the river is rolling and fertile and lies in the shadow of Clark Mountain.

In 1736, the Court of Orange County met at the home of John Branham on Spotswood land "near the Governor's Ford [Somerville] on the south side of the Rapidan," the site "being near where the

---

8. Green, "Preface."

courthouse is, with all expedition, going to be built." The plot would "include the convenientest spring to Cedar Island ford."[9] Some twenty acres were leased from Mr. Branham, and the building of the first county courthouse, a small frame structure, was accomplished by late 1738 or early 1739. Dependencies included the clerk's office, prison, pillory, whipping-post, stocks, and two ordinaries including a tavern with a separate dining room. A nearby tree west of the courthouse served as the county's hanging tree.[10]

According to Dr. A.G. Grinnan, the site of the courthouse was "on an elevated plateau south of [the Rapidan River]…overlooking for a long distance the level lands of what is now Culpeper County, lying northward [across the river]."[11]

---

9. Orange County Order Book 1, 119. W. W. Scott, 35. Ulysses P. Joyner Jr., *Glimpses of Orange County History*. Orange, VA: Orange County Historical Society, 2005, II-8.

10. Grinnan, 308. Joyner, *The First Settlers*, 134–135. Hurst, *Clark Mountain*, 135. Thomas, "Orange County Be It Remembered…," 4–5. Ann L. Miller, *Antebellum Orange: The Pre-Civil War Homes, Public Buildings, and Historic Sites of Orange County, Virginia*. Orange, VA: Orange County Historical Society, Moss Publications, 1988, 140. John Branham was issued an ordinary license in 1736. See Appendix E in Joyner, *The First Settlers*, 275. Pillory and stocks were devices made to secure criminals for public humiliation and possible further physical harm. A pillory is a device made of wood or metal erected on a post with holes for the head and hands to be secured. Pillories were related to wooden stocks which were smaller and more primitive in construction.

11. Grinnan, 308.

The courtside was located on the south side of the Rapidan River between Somerville and Raccoon Fords, just east of U.S. Highway 522 (Zachary Taylor Highway) about a half mile south of the river and the bridge on 522 crossing northward into Culpeper County. From about where Baker's Store is today on the west side of 522, the site is downhill eastward a couple of hundred yards on an elevated plateau, though the exact location of the courthouse remains in dispute.

Obviously, the courthouse needed to be on an elevated plain some distance from the Rapidan River due to flooding and for added protection there on the Virginia frontier.[12]

Reportedly, the chimneys and foundations of the courthouse complex were still visible as late as the 1930s.[13]

When Culpeper County was created from Orange County in 1749, Orange County lost more than half of its population to Culpeper County. The land area retained by Orange County included what is today Orange and Greene counties. The courthouse was suddenly alone on the northern margin of Orange County at the Orange-Culpeper county boundaries and inconvenient to most of the remaining populace of the county. Thus, the decision was made to move the courthouse to the more centrally-located rising town of Orange, the present county seat. The first Orange County Courthouse site had been utilized from 1736 (John Branham's house) until November, 1749. And, it was here that Eve's trial and execution became one of the most sensational incidents in the pre-Revolution history of Orange County.[14]

The county court was composed of some of the most distinguished citizens of Orange County, men whose reputations were deemed above reproach but also men who were landed gentry and who enjoyed the favor of the Governor at Williamsburg, and thus the Crown. They received commissions as justices of the peace, and a few of these "Gentlemen Justices" were selected to serve on the

---

12. Hurst, *Clark Mountain*, 135. Miller, *Antebellum Orange*, 140. The Hume family owned the land where the first courthouse was located circa 1907. See W. W. Scott, 36.

13. Miller, *Antebellum Orange*, 140. Thomas, "Orange County Be It Remembered," 4–5.

14. Hurst, *Clark Mountain*, 135. Joyner, *The First Settlers*, 134–135. Joyner, *Glimpses*, II-8.

county court, overseeing all cases except treason and felonies and having authority to punish offenders accordingly. White persons accused of treason and felonies were sent to Williamsburg for trial, while Blacks, presumably all slaves, were tried by special courts of Oyer and Terminer which were organized for each case and which were certified to the Governor. The Governor, in turn, commissioned a special court with four or more sworn justices. These justices, who were already justices of the county court, had the power to try slaves for treason or felony and also to extend the one-time only "benefit of clergy" to preserve literate beings should a case warrant such. They could also order proper punishment according to English law.[15]

For Eve's mid-winter trial, the commission from the Governor came on January 16, 1746, with a "dedimus potestatem" writ authorizing George Taylor and Richard Winslow to administer the oaths of office required by Parliament to the selected justices for a Court of Oyer and Terminer. Taylor and Winslow administered the "numerous oaths" to William Russell, one of the commission who, in turn, did the same for George Taylor, Richard Winslow, Edward Spencer, and Philip Clayton. The justices of the court duly sworn, Thomas Chew, the Sheriff, proclaimed that the court was duly constituted on the day of Eve's trial, January 23, 1746.[16]

---

15. Grinnan, 308-309. W. W. Scott, 136. Thomas, "Law and Medicine in Colonial Orange County," 8–9. Sparacio, 45–47. Walker, *Remembering*, 184. Slaves would sometimes be granted "benefit of clergy" for a first offense, but this plea was usually only extended the one time. At a time when ministers did most of the teaching to a mostly illiterate populace, the need to preserve those who were literate became paramount.

16. Grinnan, 308–310. Miller, *Ambrose Madison*, 67–68.

5

THE CASE OF REX V. EVE

Zachary Lewis, the King's Attorney, came before His Majesty's Justices of Oyer and Terminer on Thursday, January 23, 1746, to prosecute the case of Rex v. Eve at the first Orange County Courthouse near Somerville Ford. Again, the five "Gentleman Justices" selected and commissioned earlier on January 16th to hear the case were William Russell, George Taylor, Richard Winslow, Edward Spencer, and Philip Clayton.

The sparsely furnished courtroom was crowded that day in anticipation of a most unique trial. The five justices sat on the bench with Eve standing and facing them. She was in the custody of the Sheriff, Thomas Chew, Gentleman. As the King's Attorney addressed the court, the Clerk recorded the proceedings at his table.

The charge stated that "Eve a Negro Woman late Slave of Peter Mountague of the said County now Decd [Deceased] not having God before her Eyes nor considering the due obedience to the said Peter Mountague her Master but led and seduced by the Instigation of the Devil" had mixed a poisonous substance into the milk of her master on August 19, 1745, and that he "did most greviously languish" until December 27th of that year before finally expiring.

When King's Attorney Lewis concluded his charge against Eve, the Sheriff led her to the bar to be arraigned.[1] She pleaded that she was "in no wise thereof Guilty" and put herself upon the mercy of the court. "Diverse witnesses" were duly called, sworn, and examined, including one who came from a long distance (Caroline County) to testify. The court then "demanded of her if any thing for herself she had or knew to say why the court to judgment and execution against her of and upon the premises should not proceed, she said she had nothing to say but what she had before said." Concluding that Eve was "fully heard in her own Defence," the court rendered its judgment ["it seems to the court here..."] finding her guilty as charged. They ordered "therefore that the said Eve be Drawn upon a Hurdle [a slide or sled-like device] to the Place of Execution and there to be Burnt." The court instructed that the sentence be carried out on the "Wednesday following," January 29, when Eve was summarily burnt. Eve was judged to be worth fifty pounds and the court directed that this amount be certified to the next General Assembly. Thereupon, the court was dissolved and the proceedings were signed by the presiding judge, William Russell, January 23, 1746.[2]

Eve was charged with committing "petit," or petty treason, and pleaded not guilty. For the killing of a master by their servant—"a particularly heinous crime"—burning was a statutory punishment, especially for women.[3]

Again, slaves received no legal counsel and had to defend themselves, relying upon the mercy of the court. It does not appear that

---

1. Thomas Chew was appointed Sheriff in 1745. See Appendix L in Joyner, *The First Settlers*, 285.

2. Orange County Order Book 4, January 23, 1746, 454–455. Thomas, "Law and Medicine in Colonial Orange County," 8–9. Grinnan, 309–310. Sparacio, 45–48. Miller, *Ambrose Madison*, 67–68. Hurst, *Clark Mountain*, 132, 134–135. W. W. Scott, 135–136. Walker, *Remembering*, 183–184. Robert V. Montague III, *History and Genealogy of Peter Montague of Jamestowne, Virginia, 1603-2003*, Vol. 1, Generations 1-8, Quadricentennial Edition. Baltimore, MD: Otter Bay Books, 2013, 87–88. Joyner, *The First Settlers*, 146. Morgan, 612, 613n94.

3. Miller, *Ambrose Madison*, 67, 72. Thomas, "Law and Medicine in Colonial Orange County," 8–9. Walker, *Remembering*, 183–184. Arthur P. Scott, 194.

legal counsel was allowed any criminals in the courts of Orange County prior to the Revolution. It was after July 1776, when the officials of Orange County took oaths of allegiance to the State of Virginia, before the first mention of counsel for criminals appears in the records.[4]

English law states:

> The most heinous offense against the person known to the English law was the murder of a master by his servant. This was technically petit treason, and the punishment in England was similar to that inflicted for high treason. Offenders were dragged to the place of execution, hanged, and then quartered; women were burned instead of being hanged. Not all of the Virginia sentences included every detail of this penalty, but the distinction between petit treason and ordinary murder was always marked in some way.

Regarding English common law and burning:

> The custom in England was to strangle the victim into insensibility before the fire was lighted, and presumably this was done in Virginia also.[5]

Tully Choice was paid one hundred seventy-five pounds of tobacco, the money crop of choice, for executing Eve. He was paid another fifty pounds of tobacco for finding a sledge to draw [drag] Eve "to the place of execution." Supposedly, a hole was drilled in a rock on a hillside near the courthouse and a stake was erected for the burning. There, the sentence was summarily carried out: "the smoke of the burning of Eve was visible over a large extent of country."[6]

---

4. Grinnan, 310.

5. Arthur P. Scott, 194, 197.

6. This information is not contemporary to the case. How and where Tully Choice executed Eve is not specified in the case documents. Orange County Order Book 4, January 23, 1746, 454–455. Orange County Minute Book, October 23, 1746, 99–100. Sparacio, 48. Grinnan, 310. Philip J.

It is interesting that Eve was not burned at the Orange County Courthouse complex sitting on twenty acres. The location was known to all and the county's hanging tree was there. Everything needed to carry out the execution was available save for a high hill to maximize the spectacle.

In his book *Twice Condemned: Slaves and the Criminal Laws of Virginia, 1705-1865*, Philip Schwarz wrote:

> They also inflicted on Eve a form of execution reserved ordinarily for traitors and witches, both of whom presented an unusual threat to human power, traitors because they endangered government and witches because they supposedly had diabolical power. Eve died because of common law, her status as a slave, and her identity as a woman.[7]

With Peter Montague allegedly being poisoned to death by his servant, the "honorable justices" needed to make an example of Eve. The spectacle surrounding her burning—being dragged on a hurdle a distance from the first Orange County Courthouse up a high knoll or hillock—and then burning her at the stake so that the smoke was "visible over a large extent of country," clearly was calculated to terrorize other slaves from using "the demonstrably powerful weapon of poison" on their masters and others including other slaves. The court also wanted to deter "white conspirators who relied on slaves as accomplices in poisoning."[8]

Writing in *Murder at Montpelier: Igbo Africans in Virginia* (2005), Dr. Douglas B. Chambers contends that while whites considered milk "the ova and mala of Virginia" and drank it at every meal, the vast majority of slaves in Colonial Virginia were lactose intolerant. Thus, there was little fear of slaves drinking poisoned milk meant for whites.[9]

Schwarz, *Twice Condemned: Slaves and the Criminal Laws of Virginia, 1705-1865*. Baton Rouge, LA: Louisiana State University Press, 1988, 92.

7. Schwarz, 92.
8. Grinnan, 310. Schwarz, 92-93, 101–102. Miller, *Ambrose Madison*, 67–72.
9. Chambers, 186.

Finally, the judges did not want to make a martyr of Eve among the other slaves. In the eyes of the court, Eve was no Joan of Arc, but a conniving vindictive woman bent on destroying her master whose actions warranted this extreme form of capital punishment.

One wonders about the audience which would have assembled to witness Eve's burning, certainly a unique and unprecedented event in the county's history. Would the gathered throng have included both whites and blacks? Was Peter Montague's family present, at least his wife? Were there members of the Waugh family—perhaps, even Alexander Waugh, Sr., himself —among the crowd? Could this be how the Waugh family knew where Eve was burned (see Chapter Six)? Interestingly, no contemporary accounts of Eve's actual burning have surfaced to date.

County Supervisor and historian R. Monroe Waugh referred to Eve's burning as "the most bizarre and cruelest event in the history of Orange County." Waugh determined the site of the burning to be on his own property known as Mount Airy, where a tree was growing in the middle of a mass of large upright rocks on a knoll near the old courthouse site. Waugh named this site "Eve's Wail."[10]

In his history of Orange County, W. W. Scott stated that

> Mr. Charles S. Waugh, a venerable and highly respected citizen of Orange, remembers that his grandfather pointed out to him the little knoll near the old courthouse about Somerville's Ford where Eve was burnt. A hole was drilled in a rock and the stake inserted. Ploughing this knoll some years ago, Mr. Waugh's ploughshare slid over a rock and, recalling the narrative, he carefully scraped off the earth with his knife, and found the round hole drilled in it. There can be little doubt that this was the identical rock to which she was chained." Others claimed to have seen the metal ring which held Eve to the stake.[11]

---

10. Hurst, *Clark Mountain*, 132.
11. W. W. Scott, 135–136. Joyner, *The First Settlers*, 146.

Orange County Order Book 4 contains a detailed account of the trial, conviction, and ordered execution of Eve (see the Appendix). W. W. Scott deemed Eve's trial and burning as "the most sensational item in all the [county] records," dubbing it "a literary curiosity."[12]

Punishments in Colonial times appear barbarous by today's standards, but they reflected identical punishments in Great Britain as stipulated by English common law that governed the English colonies in America.

---

12. W.W. Scott, 135.

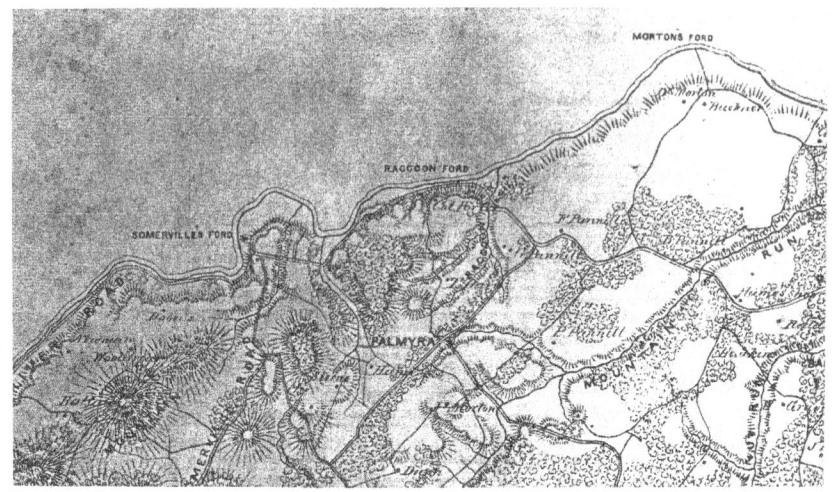

Detail from the 1864 "Gilmer Map," the Confederate Engineers' "Map of Orange," showing Somerville, Raccoon, and Morton Fords on the Rapidan River. The road running south from Raccoon Ford goes over Mount Airy, the site of Eve's burning. The area north of the river is Culpeper County. (Virginia Historical Society and the Orange Couunty Historical Society)

6

MOUNT AIRY AND THE WAUGH FAMILY

Mount Airy, the site of Eve's burning, was once part of a large tract of land belonging to Alexander Spotswood, former Lieutenant Governor of the Virginia Colony. Later, members of the Waugh Family owned much of this tract south of the Rapidan River that included Mount Airy and which extended southward to the Orange Plank Road.

Thus, just as the first Orange County Courthouse was built on lands once owned by Spotswood, so too the land encompassing Mount Airy was once part of Spotswood's massive holdings on both banks of the Rapidan River.

The present Mount Airy property is smaller today than the original tract. Now called Greenstone Farm, it has been the home of Jim and Carolyn Miller and their four children since 1996. Jim's mother, Carrie, lives with them. Since 1997, "Greenstone Farm, LLC" has produced exceptional German Warmblood Sport Horses. Today, the horse farm includes about 80 horses, some sheep, one cow, one dog, and assorted barn cats to keep down the rodents.

The Millers originally lived in the old Waugh farmhouse at the top of the high windswept hill. Later, they built their own home more sheltered on the far side of the hill next to their training facility for horses and away from the paved road down the opposite side of the long hill (Route 611, Raccoon Ford Road in Orange County).

From the crest of the hill at Mount Airy there is a spectacular panoramic view of the Rapidan River basin with the Blue Ridge Mountains in the distance.

Says Jim Miller:

> What everyone around here refers to as Clark's Mountain is just a tick west of 522 and a little south of "Mt. Airy," in other words, approximately 3 miles south west from here. It was the home of Moormont Orchards about ten years ago. I once saw (in Arizona of all places) a pre Civil War map of Virginia (I think circa about 1830, but couldn't say for sure) that actually had an area labeled "Waugh Farm" that was centered about where the Aerojet test facility (on Pine Stake Rd) is now. That would be east of Clark Mt. and South of Mt. Airy, but possibly they owned most of the area?[1]

Probably the most unique natural feature on the Mount Airy property is Haystack Rock, a massive greenstone rock shaped like a curved haystack which is surrounded by some smaller stones (Greenstone Conglomerate). An ancient site of Ice Age deposit, one wonders about the history of this place which must have witnessed everyone from the first humans in the area to Native Americans and Civil War soldiers. Was Haystack Rock ever considered a holy place, a shrine to worship? Or, perhaps, even a devil's den, a place of witchcraft? One can only speculate.[2]

Dr. Clarence Geier, a noted Civil War archaeologist and retired James Madison University professor, examined some images of Haystack Rock taken by Jim Miller for this author:

---

1. Email from Jim Miller to author, January 21, 2016. See "Moormont Orchards" at http://wikimapia.org/14966341/Moormont-Orchard-historical.

2. Hurst, *Clark Mountain*, 136.

Haystack Rock from a distance (Jim Miller)

I looked at the images and tried to enlarge them as much as possible. They are certainly unique and would probably have served as a local reference point during the historic period. My first assessment is that they are natural formations. I say that because with the magnification I have there is no evidence of having been constructed with laid stone. I'm sending these images to a friend of mine [Dr. Matt Reeves] who is the director of archaeology at Montpelier. He is well-versed in Civil War material culture and architecture. More importantly, he has been involved with studying the Confederate line on the Rapidan in the winter of 1863/1864.[3]

Dr. Matthew Reeves at Montpelier: "I agree with Clarence that the rock formation appears natural."[4]

Stanley S. Johnson, a Consulting Geologist and younger brother of Patricia J. Hurst, also looked at the images:

---

3. Email from Dr. Clarence Geier to author, January 22, 2016.
4. Email from Dr. Matt Reeves to author, January 22, 2016.

...these look natural to me. It appears that the soil has been weathered away from the more resistant rock. The rock could be diabase that is an intrusive dike. Only a field check will tell what it is for sure. Let's take a look some time.[5]

R. (Robert) Monroe Waugh (1904–1990) was a direct descendant of original immigrant Parson John Waugh (circa 1630–1706) who came to Virginia in 1660, and who was reportedly related to President James Monroe and George Mason, among others. Alexander Waugh Sr. (born before 1706, died circa 1793), a son of Parson John Waugh, and married to Sarah Battaile, was reportedly the first of the Waughs to settle on Clark Mountain in Orange County. They lived on top of the mountain, perhaps at "Mountain Side," near the Clark family. Alexander Waugh was a member of St. Thomas Parish in Orange County, serving on the vestry in 1769. He was also Justice of the Peace and Sheriff in the county, and furnished supplies to the patriots during the Revolutionary War. His family of seven children including two girls, Elizabeth and Mary, were exceedingly supportive of the cause of Liberty. Alexander and four sons served in the Revolutionary War, and a fifth son, Alexander Jr., his oldest, served in the French and Indian War. Richard was a major in the Virginia Militia; Abner, a chaplain in the Continental Army; George was a captain in the Orange County Militia; while John was a captain in the Culpeper County Militia. In 1951, the Golden Horseshoe Chapter, National Society Daughters of the American Revolution (DAR), published a memorial to perpetuate the memory of Alexander Waugh Sr., Patriot, and his family of patriots.[6]

Following General Robert E. Lee's second and last invasion of the North ending with the disastrous Gettysburg campaign in the summer of 1863, Lee's battered Army of Northern Virginia went into winter quarters in Orange County in 1863-1864 to recoup and

---

5. Email from Stan Johnson to author, March 20, 2016.

6. Hurst, *War Between the States*, 33. Richard Waugh built "Summerduck" near Raccoon Ford, and John Waugh owned a mill at Waugh's Ford (Rapidan) on the Rapidan River. Waugh Family File, Orange County Historical Society.

regroup and resupply for a spring offensive. By August, 1863, the Confederates had established their camps behind their Rapidan River defensive line—the Rapidan Line—on the high bluffs south of the river. They dug trenches and built breastworks and fortifications with artillery emplacements which extended nearly thirty miles along the river's banks—from about Rapidan Station and the Clark Mountain area eastward to at least Morton's Ford on the Rapidan. Cannon crowned the bluffs overlooking every ford on the river. Union forces occupied the northern banks of the Rapidan River which served as a natural barrier with swift currents between the opposing armies. Save for the month-long Bristoe Station campaign, Lee's army remained in Orange County until May 1864. General Lee's headquarters were near "Bloomsbury," two miles from Orange on the old and now-abandoned Orange Turnpike to Fredericksburg. Confederate President Jefferson Davis reviewed Lee's army in the spring of 1864 (historical marker near Orange). Lee, a lifelong Episcopalian, attended St. Thomas's Episcopal Church in Orange as did other Confederate notables.[7]

From the northern side of the Rapidan River, one Union observer described the Confederate defenses along the Rapidan:

> The whole line of country hereabouts is very flat, while the opposite side is a series of high hills rising one above the other from the river bank. It is all fortified and the Rebs are constantly digging on every hillside and crest…They are busy as bees throwing up entrenchments and rifle-pits. We counted sixteen guns in position on my front from Raccoon Ford up to Sommerville Ford, two miles or so…They have all the ad-

---

7. Lee's pew survives and is properly marked. A plaque on a brick wall outside commemorates the locust tree where Lee tied "Traveller," his faithful war horse. Confederate president Jefferson Davis had visited Lee and his army earlier in November 1863, and attended service at St. Thomas's. See a descriptive pamphlet entitled "The History of St. Thomas's Episcopal Church." Hurst, *Soldiers, Stories*, "Preface" and 130–131. Green, "Preface." John Mark Joseph, *War on the Rapidan*. Orange, VA: Moss Publications, 1988, 24–25.

vantages, especially as a quite high mountain back of them [Clark Mountain] serves as a lookout upon all our positions.[8]

According to Monroe Waugh, the line of Confederate breastworks running the length of the ridges in the Clark Mountain area also extended across the Mount Airy property "near Raccoon Ford." Breastworks, constituting a "fort," were dug into the hill at Mount Airy. A ditch, twelve feet wide and deep, was dug in front of these works, but the "fort" was reportedly never used. Later, a family dwelling was built over the ditch or gunpit which served as the basement of the farmhouse. The Waugh family moved into the house about the time of the First World War.[9]

According to Patricia Hurst, the Waughs living on Clark Mountain—off the present U. S. Highway 522—once put a white horse in their kitchen to hide it from the Yankees![10]

One Waugh family member who served in the Confederacy was Charles Stuart Waugh (1823–1908), then age thirty-seven or thirty-eight, who served briefly as a private in the "Orange Rangers" which became Co. "I" of the 6th Virginia Cavalry. His grandfather, Captain George Lee Waugh (1760–1814), had served in the Revolution and was at the siege of Yorktown.[11] Charles married Mary Francis Faulconer in 1847, and a son, Charles Alexander Waugh, was ten years-old when his father enlisted in the Confederate cavalry. The 1860 census lists Charles as a farmer.

Oddly, Charles Stuart Waugh was discharged on August 10, 1861, "by order of Gov. [John] Letcher," the governor of Virginia. However, he is shown as being present on the rolls in May and June 1863. Private Waugh was later assigned to a Quartermaster detachment at the supply depot in Gordonsville, Virginia. He died on

---

8. Joseph, 24–25.

9. Hurst, *Clark Mountain*, 71. Hurst, *Soldiers, Stories*, 82. Phil Audibert, "Divine Providence: The Grand Old Man of the Board of Supervisors." *Orange County Review* (May 21, 1987).

10. Hurst, *Soldiers, Stories*, 160.

11. Captain Waugh is buried near Mt. Pisgah Church, later known as Orange Chapel.

*Haystack Rock
(Jim Miller)*

The abandoned Waugh family farmhouse atop Mount Airy, now Greenstone Farm, which was built over a Confederate gunpit, part of the defense of the Rapidan Line of Lee's Army of Northern Virginia. (Jim Miller)

December 30, 1908, in Orange, and is buried in the Waugh Family Cemetery on Brush Mountain, northeast of Orange.[12]

Orange County, Virginia, like the rest of the South, was impoverished after the Civil War. As one aging Orange County planter, Jeremiah Morton of Morton Hall, surmised regarding the loss of his own fortunes as well as that of the South: "I stand a blasted stump in the wilderness of life." Morton's land tract dated from the mid-1700s and was one of the region's more prosperous farms by the time of the Civil War. A staunch secessionist, Morton sold his stately home in 1862 and invested his profits in Confederate war bonds. Morton Hall later served as Confederate Lt. General Richard S. Ewell's headquarters during the winter encampment of Lee's army in Orange County in 1863–1864. Jeremiah Morton lamented that

---

12. Courtesy of Nick Picerno's Confederate database, January 25, 2016. See also Michael P. Musick, *6th Virginia Cavalry, Virginia Regimentals.* Lynchburg, VA: H.E. Howard, Inc., 1990, 163. Waugh Family File, Orange County Historical Society. Hurst, *War Between the States*, 21.

his "delightful home and happy family of whites and blacks" had all been swept from him by "the scourge of war."[13]

Regarding Mount Airy's value as a Civil War archaeological and metal detecting site, Jim Miller offered:

> I think the Civil War activity on the site is pretty well documented and studied, which led to a *lot* of metal detecting activity and the place is pretty well picked over. I allow a couple friends of mine access but limit it to just them. They come a couple times a year, find maybe a few bullets, buttons, occasionally something a little more interesting. I don't think there is any historical information to be gained, and if there is a "big find" left I would like my friends to be the ones who stumble across it, so I'm not interested in opening it up to anyone else at this time.[14]

Monroe Waugh, his wife, Bland, and their children, Gary and Sara, lived on the "Mt. Airy Estate." His wife was the granddaughter of Colonel Samuel Bassett French (1820–1898), an attorney, judge, Confederate officer, and editor.[15]

Writing in the *Orange County Review* in 1987, staff writer Phil Audibert produced a fine feature piece on Monroe entitled "Divine Providence: The Grand Old Man of the Board of Supervisors." Monroe was then eighty-three, and his wife, Bland, had died in 1979. Monroe loved his pipe and was a long-time "friend of Tennessee whiskey," off which he was weening himself since his wife's death. At the time of the article, Monroe was living in his son Gary's house on Clark Mountain. The Waughs had moved to Mount Airy overlooking Raccoon Ford about the time of World

---

13. Miller, *Antebellum Orange*, 140–141. Joseph, 44. The property of Morton Hall is now known as Oak Green Farm and is owned by Mr. and Mrs. Richard Harris. Morton Hall itself has been dismantled and no longer exists.

14. Email from Jim Miller to the author, January 24, 2016.

15. Audibert, *Orange County Review*, May 21, 1987. Waugh Family File, Orange County Historical Society.

War I. The article mentions the site of Eve's burning as being near the water tower on the property.

Remembered Monroe Waugh:

> There's an old saying: you could walk from the Rapidan River to [Orange] Plank Road and walk on land that was owned by some damned Waugh.

He added:

> The laws of inheritance and environment are the two things that most affect you. Every person is a product of his ancestry.[16]

Monroe Waugh provided the land where the Raccoon Ford Christian Fellowship (now Riverside Church) was built, working closely with the first pastor, The Rev. David Butt. David remembers walking the property with Monroe and being fascinated by his stories about the history of Mount Airy including the story of "Eve's Wail." David does not remember being shown the site of Eve's burning.[17]

A *Richmond Times-Dispatch* obituary for R. Monroe Waugh noted that he was born October 22, 1904, in Alexandria, Virginia, the son of George Monroe and Lula Clark Waugh. Monroe was raised in Orange County. His brothers were Stiles Franklin and George Morgan Waugh. Monroe received a fine Virginia education at Randolph-Macon Military Academy in Front Royal, and Randolph-Macon College in Ashland, then two all-male schools in a state where nearly every preparatory school and college and university were once single-sex institutions. A farmer at Raccoon Ford in Orange County, Monroe served on the Board of Supervisors for thirty-two years (1948–1980) and was a representative for the Gordon District for thirty-six years (1947–1979, the year his wife died). He was chairman of the Orange County Nursing Home

---

16. Audibert, *Orange County Review*, May 21, 1987.
17. Telephone conversation with David Butt, January 18, 2016.

R. Monroe Waugh (1904–1990), who named the site "Eve's Wail" and owned Mount Airy where Eve was burned in 1746. (Orange County Historical Society)

Board of Commissioners at the time of his death, having served on their board since helping to establish the home in 1970. Monroe was fatally injured at the age of eighty-six in a car accident on Friday morning, November 23, 1990, at the intersection of Routes 636 (River Road) and 522 (near Mount Airy). He was taken to the University of Virginia Hospital in Charlottesville where he was pronounced dead. The obituary stated that Monroe was a member of St. Paul's Episcopal Church at Raccoon Ford. His wife, Sara Bland Gary Waugh, died in 1979; two children survived him, Sara and Gary (now deceased). Monroe was buried in Oakwood Cemetery in Unionville on Sunday, November 25, 1990, The Revs. David L. Butt and Anthony Busic officiating. Contributions could be sent to the Orange County Rescue Squad. The family received friends that morning at Preddy Funeral Chapel in Orange.[18]

---

18. *Richmond-Times Dispatch*, obituary, November 24, 1990. Waugh Family File, Orange County Historical Society. Telephone conversation with Sara (Waugh) Hurst of Jacksonville,

Wells Waugh, son of Gary and Sarah and Monroe's grandson, is reportedly the last of the Waughs to live on Mount Airy. "But, that was some thirty years ago," explains Wells. He did not know where Eve was burned, saying that his grandfather "told lots of stories, tales, and he drank a lot. You didn't know what to believe."[19]

Florida, March 13, 2016. Sara, a 1954 graduate of Mary Washington College in Fredericksburg, Virginia, married Army Colonel John (Jack) Hurst, a helicopter pilot in Vietnam. They retired to Florida and presently live in a retirement community in Jacksonville. Sara and historian Patricia (Pat) J. Hurst were classmates at Mary Washington. Both women married men with the surname of Hurst, but the men were not related. Pat's husband was a decorated fighter pilot in Vietnam who later died in a training accident.

19. Telephone conversation with Wells Waugh, January 14, 2016.

7

THE SITE OF "EVE'S WAIL"

There is nothing in the Orange County Order Books—the official record, if you will—that says where and how Eve was burned. It says only that "Eve was placed on a Hurdle and taken to the Place of Execution and there to be burnt." No contemporary accounts of the execution have surfaced to date. While we assume that Eve was burned at the stake, this may also be in question. The word stake is never used in the official record, though it is prescribed in the punishment phase by English law.

Ulysses P. Joyner, Pete, writing in *The First Settlers of Orange County, Virginia* (1987)—and repeating the traditional mantra (what this author calls the "Monroe Canon") says:

> A stake was duly constructed by the sheriff near the Orange County Courthouse at Raccoon Ford and the sentence of the court was carried out by burning the slave woman at the stake. There are those who claim to have seen the metal ring

which held Eve on that occasion and there is a hill near the old courthouse site referred to today as "Eve's Wail."[1]

Frank S. Walker, in *Remembering: A History of Orange County, Virginia* (2004), also states that Eve was burned at the stake, though in private conversation with this author he, too, had some doubt. Based primarily on his knowledge of what a typical burning at the stake would entail, Walker writes that

> Eve was hauled to the execution site on a hurdle (called a "slide" today), tied to the stake, and wood stacked around her. The Sheriff, Thomas Chew, threw a rope over a notch in the top of the stake and looped one end around Eve's neck. When things got too bad, he pulled on the rope, long and hard.[2]

Almost everything we know about the actual burning of Eve and the site at which it occurred comes from the recollections of several generations of the Waugh Family who lived on the Mount Airy property and neighboring properties. A venerable and well-respected "first" family of Orange County, their lands were originally part of Alexander Spotswood's massive holdings which included acreage both north and south of the Rapidan River. Alexander Waugh Sr. is the first of the family credited with living on Clark Mountain, but it is not clear as to when he settled there. However, he and other Waugh family members living in the area may well have witnessed Eve's burning.

Located off Route 611 (Raccoon Ford Road in Orange County), south of the river, the road leading up the steep drive into the property where Eve was executed today bears signage as Mt. Airy Road. The Waugh homestead here is the abandoned remains of a large two-story frame farmhouse near the crest of the hill which affords a picturesque view of the Rapidan River basin below with the Blue Ridge Mountains in the background. The property may have once

---

1. Joyner, *The First Settlers*, 146; Hurst, *Clark Mountain*, 132.
2. Walker, *Remembering*, 183–184.

extended down to the Rapidan River and westward at least to the area around U.S. Highway 522 and probably further south to about where the Aerojet Propellant Lab (Aerojet Rocketdyne) is today on Pine Stake Road. The pre-Civil War map that Jim Miller remembers seeing in Arizona identified "Waugh Farm" in the area where the Aerojet Propellant Lab is located and south of his own Mount Airy property. The identified site of Eve's burning is on a hill between U. S. Highway 522 and Route 611.

In 1986, Monroe Waugh showed Orange County historians Patricia J. Hurst and Ann L. Miller the site of "Eve's Wail" while giving them a private tour of his property. While they drove overland to the site of Eve's burning, they walked with Monroe to Haystack Rock and both ladies remember having a hard time trying to keep up with the fast-moving Mr. Waugh as they traversed Mount Airy. They also don't remember exactly where the site of Eve's burning is but both remember the eerie, foreboding, almost supernatural feeling that came over them when viewing the site. Pat felt "overwhelmed with a sense of profound grief and eeriness. It was definitely spooky." Pat Hurst took several snapshots of the site from different angles (included here) and donated them to the Orange County Historical Society in Orange. It's interesting that on the back of each snapshot she identifies the site as where Eve was burned but also adds a question mark? In her book about Clark Mountain, she also identifies the site of "Eve's Wail" writing that the burning "probably" occurred there.[3]

Pat Hurst's younger brother, Stan S. Johnson of Charlottesville, who is a Consulting Geologist, has examined the snapshots and contends that this is not a natural site. Rocks and stones shown in the images were moved from elsewhere at some point and piled there. This is typical of work clearing land for farming and livestock.[4]

Jim Miller, who also examined the images, says that the tree growing out of the mass of rocks is an "ironwood tree" known for its hardness and is indigenous to the area. Could an ancestor of

---

3. L.B. Taylor Jr., "An Event Most Cruel," *The Big Book of Virginia Ghost Stories*. Mechanicsburg, PA: Stackpole Books, 2010, 119; Hurst, *Clark Mountain*, 135.

4. Telephone conversation with Stan Johnson and Pat Hurst, March 19, 2016.

*The supposed site of Eve's burning
(Patricia J. Hurst and the Orange County Historical Society)*

this ironwood tree growing in the same spot have been the "stake" to which Eve was tied or chained? This seems more plausible than drilling a hole in a rock and then wedging in the stake.

Commenting on her snapshots, Pat Hurst feels that some of the standing stones and rocks, especially those to the right of the tree in the frontal image, appear to have been placed there purposely not only to mark the site of Eve's burning, but perhaps even to mark her grave should there have been remains.[5]

While this author is in no way attempting to refute the claims made by the good members of the Waugh family—everything they have offered may indeed be Gospel—he would like to propose an alternative sight as a possibility for the reader's edification and consideration: Haystack Rock, also on the Mount Airy property.

---

5. Telephone conversation with Pat Hurst, March 21, 2016.

*The overall site from a distance
(Patricia J. Hurst and the Orange County Historical Society)*

This huge rock, surrounded by smaller stones, is located down the backside of the of the hill from the abandoned Waugh farmhouse away from Route 611 and near the home of the Jim and Carolyn Miller family, the present owners of Mount Airy, now known as Greenstone Farm.

Shaped like a large curved haystack, Haystack Rock is a formidable and foreboding site even today, definitely unique to the present property. Studying images of Haystack Rock taken by Jim Miller, Dr. Clarence Geier, professor emeritus of James Madison University and an expert on Civil War archaeology, saw the site as a "reference point for the area back in the historic period." He also sensed that the site was natural, nothing man-made. Dr. Matt Reeves, director of archaeology at Orange County's "Montpelier," the home of James and Dolley Madison, viewed the same images and agreed with Geier that the site is, indeed, a natural one. In their

The site from a side view
(Patricia J. Hurst and the Orange County Historical Society)

presentation of the official record of Eve's trial, conviction, and sentencing—the entry in Orange County Order Book 4, pages 454–455—Ruth and Sam Sparacio, compilers and editors of *Pamunkey Neighbors of Orange County, Virginia* (1985), write that Eve was "executed by being drawn by a sledge to the place of execution, tied to a large stone and burned."[6]

From the three images of the alleged burning site included in this book—where a tree is growing from the middle of a group of large stones—none of the stones appear large enough for Eve to have been "tied to," though that particular stone may no longer exist. A lot has happened over two hundred and seventy years—not only since 1746, but since 1986, as the reader will see—and the site may very well have been compromised. However, Haystack Rock, a "reference point for the area back in the historic period," appears to be a perfect place if, indeed, Eve really was "tied to a large stone

---

6. Emails to the author from both Clarence Geier and Matt Reeves, January 22, 2016. Sparacio, 45.

*Haystack Rock from behind showing adjacent rocks
(Jim Miller)*

and burned." It would have been a place that everyone attending the spectacle of Eve's burning may have known.[7]

According to the Waugh family accounts, a hole was drilled in a rock and a wooden stake was inserted. Eve was tied or chained to the stake using a metal ring to hold her and then burned. This scenario is certainly plausible and may very well be what happened. But, what if there was no stake at all? What if Eve really was tied to a large rock—possibly, the massive Haystack Rock—and burned?

Several people I interviewed had problems with the drilled rock scenario for the stake—and in January, no less. Greenstone, which permeates the area, is a tough, dark altered basaltic rock that once was solid deep-sea lava. Thus, the Millers named their Mount Airy property Greenstone Farm after this hard rock.

Alec Waugh, clinging to the traditional mantra, mused that at the rock outcropping where Eve was burned the stake would have

---

7. Email from Clarence Geier to the author, January 22, 2016. Sparacio, 45.

been green wood so that it wouldn't burn before Eve burned. Also, he felt that the hole drilled in the rock must have been large.[8]

Questioning the "Monroe Canon," historian and author Frank S. Walker, a former farmer, said:

> ...to erect a stake you don't drill a hole in a rock and then try to wedge a stake of some girth into that hole. You dig a hole in the ground, place the stake in it, and cover it with dirt and rock to support it and keep it stable.[9]

Jim Miller:

> I will poke around and send pictures when I get a chance, but that area is pretty overgrown. Should be able to narrow it down based on the '86 pictures. We arrived in '96 and have a pretty good feel for what has changed, what trees fell, etc. I'm still pretty dubious as to the hole in the rock, just seems like an awful lot of effort and expense, particularly given how hard the rock is around here and the fact that the drilling would have been done by hand…but, who knows…Oral history can be very interesting, but unfortunately can be as unreliable as a laundered cell phone.[10]

At any rate, the late R. Monroe Waugh often said that if the property including the burning site—which was reportedly between the old water tower on his property and the present Riverside Church—were ever developed, he wanted one of the streets to be named "Eve's Wail."[11]

Jim Miller again:

---

8. Telephone conversation with Alec Waugh, January 13, 2016.
9. Telephone conversation with Frank S. Walker, January 15, 2016.
10. Email from Jim Miller to the author, January 19, 2016. Jim's cell phone *was* laundered!
11. Walker, *Remembering*, 184.

Regarding the water tower, it is still in place (the tank is long gone but the old steel tower is still there) and there were rock outcroppings on the northwest face of that hill. Nothing that would come close to the descriptions of a rock that a person could be tied to, but lots of boulders just peeking out of the ground that we removed for ease of pasture maintenance. If you go on the premise that Eve may have been burned at an actual stake, possibly near a large rock, then it seems reasonable that that northwest hill face could be where one might place a stake. Sometime when the weather is better and the ground is firmer I'll show you that general area.[12]

Sara (Waugh) Hurst, Monroe's eighty-three year-old daughter who lives in Florida, doesn't remember the location of Eve's execution. She remembered that her father talked about Eve's burning many times, but she did not remember the site being near the water tower which is also near the Waugh farmhouse, her home. When Sara began talking about Eve with this author there was some confusion and it is possible that her recollection is confused with other stories Monroe told his family and friends.[13]

On Monday, February 29, 2016 (leap year), this author made a physical inspection of the area from near the abandoned Waugh farmhouse at the crest of Mount Airy down to the Riverside Church near the bottom of the long, steep hill off Route 611 (Raccoon Ford Road in Orange County). One can almost draw a straight line between the Waugh farmhouse and the church. For nearly four hours, I walked the steep wooded property armed only with my Vermont walking stick, a disposable camera, and a photocopy of the three snapshots from 1986 reportedly showing the burning site. I had parked in the church parking lot and taped a note to my windshield. There were a couple of other cars there, so I went inside the church and introduced myself to John Fogle, the pastor, who was working with some others. He knew about Eve's burning

---

12. Email from Jim Miller to the author, February 2, 2016.
13. Telephone conversation with Sara Waugh Hurst, March 13, 2016.

Riverside Church, formerly the Raccoon Ford Christian Fellowship, located near the foot of the old Mount Airy property. Eve was reportedly burned somewhere between the old water tower on the property and the church. (Pastor John Fogle, Riverside Church)

from the former pastor there, David Butt, when it was the Raccoon Ford Christian Fellowship. John didn't know where the site was either, but gave me his blessing to search wherever I wanted and for as long as I wanted.

I decided to save the church property for last and started working my way up the steep terrain into the adjoining ten acres (now owned by Bridget Buddenberg) and finally to the Miller property itself. Unexpectedly, I saw Jim Miller working up ahead with the Waugh farmhouse framed in the background. As always, Jim was very accommodating, opening gates and turning off electric fences for me to have full access to the wooded property. Over the next few hours, I made friends with two young horses (on a farm with 80 horses) who wanted to play; surprised a beautiful doe and her pretty little fawn; and enjoyed the red fox that ran across my path. I inspected every boulder and rock I spotted including the trees around them, if any. A couple of places looked more like where the burning may have taken place than the site depicted in the

*Site of the old water tower on the Mount Airy property
(now Greenstone Farm), located near the Waugh farmhouse.
The site of Eve's burning is reportedly nearby.
(Jim Miller)*

snapshots. Coming back down the hill, I inspected the area around the Riverside Church including the land behind the church and fronting on U.S. Highway 522, a tract owned by musician Billy Cooper. However, by the end of my journey, I did not find any site that came close to matching the snapshots.

Jim Miller said that in the years up to and including his buying and moving to Mount Airy in 1996, that a lot of work has been done to open up the property for horses with their safety being paramount. Some trees fell, perhaps even the "ironwood tree" at the site of Eve's burning, large boulders and stones were removed, and underbrush cleared away. I saw a large pile of boulders and stones that had been removed from various areas of the property. In short, it may well be that the site depicted in the 1986 snapshots—just twenty years ago—has either been obliterated or compromised to the point that it is unrecognizable. The snapshots may be all the evidence that we have. And, perhaps, that is for the best anyway. With no site to mark and visit, no shrine or cult to develop, the slave Eve and the land that once was Mount Airy can remain at peace from that horrible day in 1746.

After inspecting all the property that I could and finding nothing, I bid Jim Miller and John Fogle goodbye and prepared to leave. Worn out, dirty, and hungry, my sixty-five year-old body aching all over, I got into my vehicle and started down the winding gravel road from the church. Out of the corner of my right eye I spotted a horse in the distance coming out of the woods and up to the electric fence. I had looked over at that area earlier and there were no horses present. As I came around to as close as I could to the horse, I stopped and rolled down my passenger side window. Though still a fair distance from the animal, I could see that she was a powerful-looking mare, a magnificent beast. She seemed to be looking right at me and I stared back in awe. Something, I can't explain what, passed between us. She seemed to know what I was about, what I was looking for, and that I hadn't found that terrible place. We stared at each other briefly when suddenly it hit me…

EPILOGUE

The burning of Eve in Virginia was not the first nor the last of the court ordered burnings at the stake in the English colonies in America. However, according to Orange County historian Frank S. Walker Jr.: "There were relatively few executions by burning at the stake in Virginia."[1]

Eve was not even the first reported slave burned at the stake in the Virginia Colony. In February 1736/37, an unidentified female slave in Nansemond County (now the independent city of Suffolk, Virginia), was burned for murdering her mistress with a broad ax. She reportedly confessed and was charged with "petit treason." That in both cases the slaves were women, supposedly the weaker sex, is probably indicative of the court's vengeance against them.[2]

1. Walker, *Remembering*, 184 (note 16).
2. Schwarz, 81.

Writing in the January 1896 issue (Vol. III, No. 3) of *The Virginia Magazine of History and Biography*, a publication of the Virginia Historical Society in Richmond, Dr. A.G. Grinnan incorrectly surmised that, in addition to Eve's burning, there were only two other known "cases in which criminals have been burnt at the stake by judicial process in the region now embraced by the United States during the Colonial period." According to Grinnan, in 1610–1611, a man was burned at the stake in Jamestown, Virginia, for killing and eating his wife; and a female slave was similarly burned in 1749 in Cambridge, Massachusetts, for murdering her master. Grinnan's article "The Burning of Eve in Virginia" was included in the "Historical Notes and Queries" section of the magazine.[3]

The hysteria surrounding the fear of black poisonings that permeated the Southern colonies was unusually high in South Carolina. In 1741, a "Negro Doctor" allegedly poisoned a white infant and was burned at the stake. Executions for such crimes included "burning, gibbeting, [and] hanging." In 1761, slaves had reportedly "begun again the hellish practice of poisoning," and "whites retaliated savagely, gibbeting and burning alive the suspects."[4]

Dr. Jeff Bach, Director of the Young Center for Anabaptist and Pietist Studies at Elizabethtown College in Pennsylvania:

> Supposedly, there was a woman burned at the stake in Philadelphia in the late 1730s for joining her youthful lover to kill her husband. Her case was tried as treason, rather than adultery. Her execution at the stake was reported by Ben Franklin in his newspaper. But some people have told me that his newspaper was guilty of exaggerating and creating stories, so I don't know if it's really true. I need to do some legal research. But I'm very interested to know if any other colonies

---

3. Grinnan, 308–310.

4. Morgan, 613. Gibbeting refers to a gallows-type structure with a projecting arm at the top from which dead or dying bodies of criminals were hung for public display, often for long periods of time. The term "gibbet" may also refer to placing a criminal within a gibbet, sometimes called "hanging in chains."

had courts that actually ordered a burning at the stake as a judicial punishment.[5]

Two known cases of burning at the stake took place in Massachusetts. In 1681, a slave named Maria was convicted of arson for trying to kill her master by setting his house on fire. She was burned at the stake in Roxbury, now a Boston neighborhood. Concurrently, Jack, a slave convicted in a separate arson case, was hanged nearby and his body thrown into the fire with that of Maria. In 1755 in Cambridge, across the Charles River from Boston, slaves Mark and Phillis were executed for murdering their owner. He was hanged and his body gibbeted, while she was burned at the stake.

In the early eighteenth-century, New York had one of the largest slave populations of any of the English colonies in America, though there was no plantation system like in the Southern colonies. Constant fear of slave revolts led to a large number of burnings at the stake between 1708 and 1741, for example. In 1712, some twenty people were burnt following a slave revolt, while in 1741, at least thirteen slaves were burned at the stake following an alleged slave conspiracy.[6]

Frank S. Walker Jr. in *Remembering: A History of Orange County, Virginia* (2004) noted that in New York City in 1714, twenty-nine slaves involved in a series of arsons and lootings were sentenced to be burned or hanged.[7]

Thus, Eve's burning at the stake in Virginia was one of many such punishments ordered by the judicial systems in Colonial America as prescribed by English law. She apparently received a fair trial for the time. There were witnesses for the prosecution and Eve, not having legal representation, was allowed to testify on her own behalf and to throw herself upon the mercy of the court. The court showed no mercy, not even extending "benefit of clergy."

---

5. Email from Jeff Bach to the author, February 1, 2016.
6. See https://en.wikipedia.org/wiki/Death_by_burning#North_America.
7. Walker, *Remembering*, 184 (note 16).

It's all gone now, the first Orange County Courthouse and probably even the site of Eve's burning on the land once known as Mount Airy. The present Greenstone Farm, with its splendid view of the area, is a haven for horses-in-training and other assorted critters, and is lovingly worked daily by the Miller family.

In closing, one prays that Eve's soul is at peace, but one also wonders?

APPENDIX

Here is a transcription of pages 454–455 in Orange County Order Book 4, courtesy of the Orange County Circuit Court, Orange, Virginia. See also Ruth Trickey and Sam Sparacio, compilers and editors, *Pamunkey Neighbors of Orange County, Virginia* (Baltimore, MD: Gateway Press, Inc., 1985), 45–47.

Rex v. Eve

23 January 1745/46, Orange County, Virginia

Memorandum. That at the court house of Orange County on Thursday the 23 day of January in the nineteenth year of the reign of George the Second, by Grace of God of Great Britain, ye Anno Domino 1745, his Majesty's commission and the seal of this colony and dominion of Virginia, bearing date this day of this instant directed to Robert Slaughter, Abraham Field, Robert Green, James Barbour, John Tinlaw, Samuel Ball, Francis Slaughter, James Pollard, Robert Eastham, Zachary Taylor, Benjamin Cave, Charles

Curtis, William Russell, James Coleman, George Taylor, Richard Winslow, William Triplett, Henry Field, Edward Spencer, Richard Thomas, Joseph Thomas, Goodrich Lightfoot, Philip Clayborn, James Pendleton, Peter Sholl, Gentlemen, or any four of them, whereof Robert Slaughter, Abraham Field, Robert Green, James Barbour, John Tinlaw, Samuel Ball, Francis Slaughter, James Pollard, Robert Eastham, Zachary Taylor, Benjamin Cave, Charles Curtis, William Russell and James Coleman should be one to hear and determine all treason, petit treason, or misprisons whereof, felonies, murders and other offenses or crimes whatsoever committed or perpetrated within this county by Eve, a negro woman slave, lately belonging to Peter Mountague, was openly as was in like manner his Majesty's dedimus potestatem under the said seal of the same role for administering the oath before God to the said commissioners, by virtue of which the said George Taylor and Richard Winslow administered the oath appointed by Acts of Parliament to be taken instead of the oaths of Allegiance and Supremacy, the Abjuration Oath, and unto the said William Russell, who subscribed the same Abjuration Oath and Test, and then the said George Taylor and Richard Winslow likewise administered to him the oath of a Justice of Oyer and Terminer, and the said William Russell thereupon administered the oaths appointed by Act of Parliament to be taken instead of the oaths of Allegiance and Supremacy, the said Abjuration Oath in both and Test unto the said George Taylor, Richard Winslow, Edward Spencer and Philip Clayborn, who also subscribed the said last mentioned oath and test, and then the said William Russell likewise administered the said George Taylor, Richard Winslow, Edward Spencer and Philip Clayborn the oath of a Justice of Oyer and Terminer.

The court being thus constituted, Zachary Lewis, Gent., attorney for our Sovereign Lord, the King, in the court of the county aforesaid, comes here into court before the said William Russell, George Taylor, Richard Winslow, Edward Spencer and Philip Clayborn, his Majesties Justices of Oyer and Terminer, for the said county by special commission appointed to hear and determine all freeman's petit furiositatem or misprisons thereof, felonious murders, or other offenses or crimes whatsoever committed or perpetrated within the county aforesaid, by Eve, a negro woman slave, lately belonging to Peter Mountague, the 23d day of January in the nineteenth year of the reign of our sovereign Lord, George the Second, now King of Great Britain, ye in his proper person and form, said Lord, the King, gives this court to understand, and be informed, that Eve, a negro woman, late slave of Peter Mountague of the said county, and she not having God before her eyes nor considering the one obedient to the said Peter Mountague, her master, but did said induced by the instigation of the Devil, the nineteenth day of August in the year of our Lord 1745 at the county aforesaid with force and arms of her malice aforethought, certain milk with deadly poison, that is to say, feloniously and haiterously did mingle and poison and the same milk so mixt, corrupt and poisoned, then and there feloniously and haiterously did give the said Peter Mountague, then her master, which said Peter Mountague, not fearing or distrusting the mixture, corruption or poison aforesaid, the same milk with the poison aforesaid by the said Eve as poisoned by the procurement and instigation of the said Eve, and there did eat, drink and swallow down of which said milk is with the said poison aforesaid mingled, poisoned and received the aforesaid Peter Mountague did most grievously languish from the aforesaid nineteenth day of August in the year aforesaid until the twenty seventh day of December in the year aforesaid, the said Peter Mountague so mortally poisoned with the poison aforesaid, died, and so aforesaid Eve, the aforesaid Peter Mountague, her late master, falsely, traitorously and feloniously of her mallice aforethought with the poison aforesaid kill, poison and murder, contrary to the form of the statute and against the peace.

Whereupon the said Eve was instantly lead to the bar under the custody of Thomas Chew, Gentl., sheriff of the county aforesaid, to whose custody before for the causes aforesaid she was committed, and being arraigned of the premises, she said she was in no wise thereof guilty, and thereof according to the form of the Act of the General Assembly in cases of this nature, made and provided she did not put herself upon the court upon which diverse witnesses were produced, sworn and examined against the said Eve, and she fully heard in her own defense, whereupon it seems to the court here that the said Eve is guilty of murder aforesaid, in manner and form as above against her is alledged, and it being demanded of her if any thing for herself she had or knew to say why the court to judgment and execution against her of and upon the premises should not proceed, she said she had nothing to say but what she had before said.

Therefore it is considered by the court that the said Eve be drawn upon a hurdle to the place of execution and there to be burnt, and it is said to the sheriff that execution thereof be done on Wednesday next, and the court to be adjudged the said Eve to be of the value of fifty pounds, which is ordered to be certified to the next session of the Assembly.

On the motion of Hugh Noden, Gent., a witness for our Sovereign Lord, the King, against Eve, a negro woman, late slave of Peter Mountague, dec'd, it is ordered that it be certified to the next session of the Assembly that he has come fifty miles out of Caroline County and hath attended one day at a court of Oyer and Terminer held for the trial of the said Eve.

The minutes of these proceedings were signed.

W. Russell

BIBLIOGRAPHY

Audibert, Phil. "Divine Providence: The Grand Old Man of the Board of Supervisors." *County Living, Orange County Review* (Thursday, May 21, 1987), B-1.

Bouvier, John. *A Law Dictionary, Adapted to the Constitution and Laws of the United States…* Philadelphia, PA: Childs and Peterson, 1856.

Chambers, Douglas B. *Murder at Montpelier: Igbo Africans in Virginia*. Jackson, MS: University Press of Mississippi, 2005.

Chumbley, George Lewis. *Colonial Justice in Virginia: The Development of a Judicial System, Typical Laws and Cases of the Period*. Richmond, VA: The Dietz Press, 1938.

Dorman, John Frederick. *Adventurers of Purse and Person: Virginia 1607-1624/5*. 4th edition, Vol. 2. Baltimore, MD: Genealogical Publishing Company, 2004–2007.

Green, James William. *Orange Court House, 1861–1865*. Published by the Orange County Civil War Centennial Committee. Orange, VA: Printed by *The Orange Review*, 1965.

Grinnan, Dr. A.G. "The Burning of Eve in Virginia." *The Virginia Magazine of History and Biography*. Vol. III, No. 3 (January 1896), 308–310.

Hening, William Waller. *The Statutes at Large: Being a Collection of All the Laws of Virginia…* Vol. VI. Published For the Jamestown Foundation of the Commonwealth of Virginia. Charlottesville, VA: The University Press of Virginia, 1969, 105.

"The History of St. Thomas's Episcopal Church." Orange, VA (Descriptive pamphlet).

Hurst, Patricia J. *The History and People of Clark Mountain, Orange County, Virginia*. Rapidan, VA: P.J. Hurst, 1989.

Hurst, Patricia J. *Soldiers, Stories, Sites, and Fights, Orange County, Virginia, 1861–1865, and the Aftermath*. Rapidan, VA: P.J. Hurst, 1998.

Hurst, Patricia J. *The War Between the States, 1862–65: Rapidan River Area of Clark Mountain, Orange County, Virginia*. Rapidan, VA: P.J. Hurst, 1989.

Jester, Annie Lash and Martha Woodroof Hiden. *Adventurers of Purse and Person: Virginia, 1607–1625*. Order of First Families of Virginia, 1607–1620. Princeton, NJ: Princeton University Press, 1956.

Joseph, John Mark. *War on the Rapidan*. Orange, VA: Moss Publications, 1988.

Joyner, Ulysses P. Jr. *The First Settlers of Orange County, Virginia*. Baltimore, MD: Published for the Orange County Historical Society by Gateway Press, Inc., 1987.

Joyner, Ulysses P. Jr. *Glimpses of Orange County History*. Orange, VA: Orange County Historical Society, 2005.

Maass, John R. *The Road to Yorktown: Jefferson, Lafayette and the British Invasion of Virginia*. Charleston, SC: The History Press, 2015.

Meyer, Virginia M. and John Frederick Dorman. *Adventurers of Purse and Person, Virginia, 1607–1624/5*. 3rd ed., revised and edited. Order of First Families of Virginia, 1607–1624/5. Richmond, VA: The Dietz Press, Inc., 1987.

Miller, Ann L. *Antebellum Orange: The Pre-Civil War Homes, Public Buildings, and Historic Sites of Orange County, Virginia*. Orange, VA: Orange County Historical Society (Moss Publications), 1988.

Miller, Ann L. *The Short Life and Strange Death of Ambrose Madison*. Orange, VA: Orange County Historical Society, 2001.

Montague, George William. *History and Genealogy of Peter Montague, of Nansemond and Lancaster Counties, Virginia, and his descendants, 1621–1894*. Amherst, MA: Press of Carpenter & Morehouse, 1894.

Montague III, Robert V. *History and Genealogy of Peter Montague of Jamestowne Colony, Virginia (The First Three Generations)*. 1st ed. Navarre, FL: R. V. Montague III, 2003.

Montague III, Robert V. *History and Genealogy of Peter Montague of Jamestowne, Virginia, 1603–2003*. Vol. 1, Generations 1–8, Quadricentennial Edition. Baltimore, MD: Otter Bay Books, 2013.

Morgan, Philip D. *Slave Counterpoint: Black Culture in the Eighteenth-Century Chesapeake & Low Country*. Published for the Omohundro Institute of Early American History and Culture, Williamsburg, Virginia. Chapel Hill, NC: The University of North Carolina Press, 1998.

Musick, Michael P. *6th Virginia Cavalry*. Virginia Regimental Histories Series. Lynchburg, VA: H.E. Howard, Inc., 1990.

Schwarz, Philip J. *Twice Condemned: Slaves and the Criminal Laws of Virginia, 1705–1865*. Baton Rouge, LA: Louisiana State University Press, 1988.

Scott, Arthur P. *Criminal Law in Colonial Virginia*. Chicago, IL: The University of Chicago Press, 1930.

Scott, W. W. *A History of Orange County, Virginia*. Richmond, VA: Everett Waddey Co., 1907.

Sparacio, Ruth Trickey and Sam, compilers and editors. *Pamunkey Neighbors of Orange County, Virginia*. Baltimore, MD: Gateway Press, Inc., 1985.

Swem, Earl Gregg. *Virginia Historical Index*. Vol. II (L–P). Gloucester, MA: Peter Smith, 1965 (reprint).

Thomas, William H.B. "Law and Medicine in Colonial Orange County." *Bicentennial Series #3* (July 1975), 8–9. Orange County Bicentennial Commission. Orange, VA: Printed by Green Publishers, Inc.

Thomas, William H.B. "Orange County Be It Remembered…" *Bicentennial Series # 1* (January 1975), 4–5, 8–9. Orange County Bicentennial Commission. Orange, VA: Printed by Green Publishers, Inc.

Walker, Frank S. Jr. *Echoes of Orange*. Orange, VA: Orange County Historical Society, 2013.

Walker, Frank S. Jr. *Remembering: A History of Orange County, Virginia*. Orange, VA: Orange County Historical Society, 2004.

Yurechko, John Otto. *Christ Church Parish Register, Middlesex County, Virginia, 1553–1812*. Westminster, MD: Family Line Publications, 1996.

Primary Sources

Confederate Database (Nicholas P. Picerno), Bridgewater, Virginia
Orange County Circuit Court, Orange, Virginia
    Deed Book 10
    Minute Book
    Order Book 1, 2, 4, 5
    Will Book 2, 3
Orange County Historical Society, Orange, Virginia
    Library Collection
    Waugh Family File
    Montague Family File
    Montague-Stevens Family File
Spotsylvania County Circuit Court, Spotsylvania Courthouse, Virginia
    Deed Book D

Newspapers

Orange County Review, May 21, 1987
Richmond-Times Dispatch, November 24, 1990

Calendar (Julian, Old Style; Gregorian, New Style)

https://search.yahoo.com/search;_ylt=AnqdNH4dSu8Y_RMRcO6Ft..bvZx4?p=English+Old+Style+and+New+Style+calendars&toggle=1&cop=mss&ei=UTF-8&fr=yfp-t-901&fp=1.

Libraries, Historical Societies, and Museums

Bridgewater College, Bridgewater, Virginia
    Alexander Mack Memorial Library
    Archives and Special Collections
    Reuel B. Pritchett Museum
James Madison Museum of Orange County History, Orange, Virginia
Norfolk Public Library, Norfolk, Virginia
    Sargeant Memorial Local History and Genealogy Collection
Orange County Historical Society, Orange, Virginia
Orange County Public Library, Orange, Virginia
    Local History and Genealogy
Rockbridge Regional Library, Lexington, Virginia
    Local History and Genealogy
    Interlibrary Loan
University of Virginia, Charlottesville, Virginia
    Alderman Library
University of the South, Sewanee, Tennessee
    DuPont Library
Virginia Military Institute, Lexington, Virginia
    Preston Library
Washington and Lee University, Lexington, Virginia
    Leyburn Library

Special Collections and Archives
Law Library

Maps

Confederate Engineer's Map: 1864 "Gilmer Map," actually entitled "Map of Orange," from Major General J.F. Gilmer, Chief Engineer, D.N.V., Confederate Engineer's Bureau, Richmond, VA. Made under the direction of A. H. Campbell, Captain, Engineers, in charge of the Topographical Department. The original is in the Virginia Historical Society, Richmond, and the Orange County Historical Society sells facsimiles.

Virginia Topographical Maps http://www.mytopo.com/Virginia
   Mine Run
   Unionville

Websites

Montague, Peter (1718–1745): www.werelate.org/wiki/Person:
Moormont Orchards, Clark Mountain, Orange County, VA: http://wikimapia.org/14966341/Moormont-Orchard-historical.

Interviews: In-Person, Email and Telephone

Jeff Bach	Clarence Geier
Jayne E. Blair	Carrie Heitsch
Bridget Buddenberg	Patricia J. Hurst
David Butt	Sarah (Waugh) Hurst
Billy Cooper	Stan Johnson
John Fogle	Jean McGann

Leslie McGowan

Karin Merrill

Ann L. Miller

Jim and Carolyn Miller

Nick Picerno

Matt Reeves

Walker Somerville

Bethany Sullivan

Troy Valos

Frank S. Walker Jr.

Alec Waugh

Sarah Waugh

Wells Waugh

INDEX

A

Abjuration Oath and Test, 62
Act of 1748 (1748 Act), 16
Acts of Parliament (British), 11, 62
Act of the General Assembly, Williamsburg, VA, 63
Aerojet Propellant Lab (Aerojet Rocketdyne), 34, 47
African Americans (Negroes, Blacks), 12, 15–17, 29
"African medicine," 3, 16
Albemarle County, VA, 18
Alexandria, VA, 42
Allegheny Mountains, 19
Allegiance and Supremacy, Oath of, 62
Allen, Ellenor (Mountague), 7
Arc, Joan of, xi, 30
Archaeology, 34–35, 41, 49
Arizona, 34, 47
Army of Northern Virginia (CSA), 36, 40
Ashland, VA, 42
Audibert, Phil, 41
Augusta County, VA, 19

B

Bach, Jeff, 19, 58
Baker's Store, 24
Ball, Samuel, 61
Barbour, James, 61
Battaile, Sarah (Waugh), 36
Baylor, John, 16
"Benefit of Clergy," 16, 25, 59
Blacks (African Americans), 12, 15–17, 29
Blacks (African Americans), Free, 12, 16

73

"Bloomsbury," 37
Blue Ridge Mountains (Great Mountains), 17, 19, 21–22, 34, 46
Board of Commissioners, Orange County Nursing Home, 42–43
Board of Supervisors, Orange County, VA, 42
Boston, MA, 59
Branham, John, 22–24
Bristoe Station (VA) campaign, 1863, 37
British, 20
British Parliament, 11, 62
Brush Mountain, 40
Buddenberg, Bridget, 54
Burning at the Stake, 27–28, 30, 32–33, 42–48, 50–60, 64
"The Burning of Eve in Virginia," VMHB (1896), 19, 58
Busic, Anthony, 43
Butt, David, 42–43, 54

C

Cambridge, MA, 58–59
Caroline County, VA, 4, 27, 64
Cave, Benjamin, 61
Cedar Mountain, Battle of, 21
Cedar Run, 23
Cedar Island Ford, 23
Census, 1860, 38
Chambers, Douglas B., 29
Charles (ship), 7
Charles River, 59
Charlottesville, VA, 18, 43, 47
Chestnut Mountain (Clark Mountain), 13, 21
Chew, Thomas, 25–27, 46, 63
Choice, Tully, 28
Christ Church Parish, Middlesex County, VA, 8

Civil law, England, 11
Civil War, The, 20, 22, 40–41
Civil War archaeology, 34–35, 41, 49
Civil War soldiers, 34
Clark Family (Clark Mountain), 36
Clark Mountain (Chestnut Mountain), 13, 21–22, 34, 36–38, 41, 46–47
Clayborn, Philip, 62
Clayton, Philip, 25–26
Clerk, Orange County Court, VA, 26
Coleman, James, 62
Common Law, English, 11
Commonwealth of Virginia, 18
Company "I," 6th Virginia Cavalry, 38
Confederacy, The, 21, 38
Confederate Army, 21, 32, 37–38
Confederate Bonds (War), 40
"Conjure" (poison), 4, 12, 15–16
Consulting Geologist, 35, 47
Continental Army, 36
Cooper, Billy, 56
Country doctors, slaves as, 3–4, 16
Court of Oyer and Terminer, xi, 14–15, 25–26
Crown (British), 24
Culpeper County, VA, 18–21, 23–24, 32
Culpeper County Militia, 36
Curtis, Charles, 61

D

Daniel, James, 10
Daniel, Reuben, 10
Daughters of the American Revolution (DAR), 36
Davis, Jefferson, 37
"Dedimus Potestatem" writ (Commission), 25, 62
Devil's den, 34

Disembolweling, 11
"Diverse witnesses," 4, 27, 63
"Divine Providence: The Grand Old Man…" (1987), 41

E

Eastham, Robert, 61
Elizabethtown College, 19, 58
"Enchanted Castle," 19
England, 14, 18, 28
English, 14, 18, 28, 31
English Colonies, xi, 11, 28, 31, 57, 59
English Common Law, xi, 11, 25, 28–29, 31, 45, 59
Episcopalians, 37
Essex County, VA, 8
Eve (slave), xi–xiii, 3–5, 8-9, 14–20, 22, 24–33, 42–64
Eve's burning, site of, xiii, 30, 42–48, 50–64
Eve's grave? 48
"Eve's Wail," xiii, 30, 42–43, 46–48, 52
"Eve's Wail," possible street name? 52
Ewell, Richard S., 40

F

Faulconer, Mary Frances (Waugh), 38
Felony, xi, 25, 62
Field, Abraham, 61
Field, Henry, 62
The First Settlers of Orange County, Virginia (1987), 45
First World War, 38, 41–42
Florida, 44, 53
Fogle, John, 53–54, 56
France, xi, 19
Franklin, Benjamin, 58

French and Indian War, 36
Fredericksburg, VA, 37, 44
French, xi, 19–20
French, Samuel Bassett, 41
Front Royal, VA, 42

G

Geier, Clarence, 34, 49
General Assembly, Williamsburg, VA, 27, 64
"Gentleman Justices," 24, 26
George II, King of England, 61, 63
German Warmblood Sport Horses, 33
Germanna, 18–19
Germanna Ford, 18–19
Germans, 19
Germany, 19
Gettysburg (PA) campaign, 1863, 36
Gibbet and Gibbeting, 58–59
"Gilmer Map" (1864), 32
Golden Horseshoe Chapter, DAR, 36
Goodwin, Mrs. Dr. J. Minor, 9
Gordon District, VA, 42
Gordonsville, VA, 38
Governor, Virginia Colony, Williamsburg, 24–25
"The Governor's Ford" (Somerville Ford), 20, 22
Great Britain, 31
Great Lakes, 19
Great Mountains (Blue Ridge Mountains), 19, 21, 34, 46
Green, Robert, 61
Greene County, VA, 18–19, 24
Greenstone, 34, 51
Greenstone Conglomerate, 34–36
Greenstone Farm, 33, 40, 49, 51, 55, 60
"Greenstone Farm, LLC," 33
Grinnan, A.G., 15, 19, 23, 58

H

"Hanging in chains" (Gibbet), 58
Hanging Tree, Orange County, 23, 29
Harris, Richard (Mr. and Mrs.), 41
Haystack Rock, 34–35, 39, 47–51
Heitsch, Carrie, 33
High Treason, 11-12, 28, 62
"Historical Notes and Queries," VMHB (1896), 58
A History of Orange County, Virginia (1907), 14, 30–31
Hume Family, 24
Hurdle (slide, sled-like device), 27–28, 45–46, 50, 64
Hurst, John (Jack), 44
Hurst, Patricia J. (Pat), 13, 35, 38, 44, 47–50
Hurst, Sara Waugh, 43–44, 53

I

Ice Age, 34
Igbo Africans, 4
Illiteracy, 25
Indians (Native Americans), 17–18, 34
"Insult to the body" (poisoning), 15
"Ironwood tree," 47–48, 56

J

Jack (slave), 59
Jacksonville, FL, 43–44
James Madison University, 34, 49
Jamestown, VA, 58
Joan of Arc, xi, 30
Johnson, Stanley S., 35, 47
Joyner, Ulysses P., 45
Justice of Oyer and Terminer, Oath of, 14, 62

Justices of the Peace, Orange County, VA, 14, 24, 36

K

King's Attorney, 26–27, 62

L

Lafayette, Marquis de, 20–21
Lancaster County, VA, 8
Legal counsel, lack of, 27
Lee, Robert E., 36–37, 40
Letcher, John, 38
Letty (Slave), 14–15
Lewis, Zachary, King's Attorney, 26–27, 62
Lightfoot, Goodrich, 62
Little Mountains (Southwest Mountains), 21
Louisa County, VA, 18

M

Maass, John R., 21
Madison, Ambrose, 12–13
Madison, Dolley, 49
Madison, Frances Taylor, 13
Madison, James, 49
Madison County, VA, 15, 18–19
"Map of Orange" (1864), 32
Maria (slave), 59
Mark (slave), 59
Mary Washington College, 44
Mason, George, 36
Massachusetts, 59
Medicinal "cures," 3–4, 16, 58
Metal detecting, 41
Middlesex County, VA, 8, 14
Milk, poisoned, 29–30, 63
Miller, Ann L., 15, 47

Miller, Carolyn, 33, 49, 51, 54, 60
Miller, Jim, 33–35, 39–41, 47, 49, 51–56, 60
Mississippi River, 19
Monroe, James, 36
"Monroe Canon," 45, 51–52
"Montpelier," 4, 12, 35, 49
Moormont Orchards, 34
Morton, Jeremiah, 40
Morton Ford, 32, 37
Morton Hall, 40–41
"Mount Airy," 20, 22, 30, 32–34, 38, 40–44, 46–49, 51, 53–56, 60
"Mount Pleasant" ("Montpelier"), 12
Mountague (Montague), Anthorit, 4, 8–10, 30
Mountague (Montague), Elizabeth, 4, 8, 10
Mountague, Ellenor (Allen), 7
Mountague (Montague) Family, 3–10, 17
Mountague (Montague), Grace, 8
Mountague (Montague), Peter (son of Peter of Boveny), 7
Mountague (Montague), Peter, Junior (1718–1745), xii, xiii, 3–5, 7–10, 17, 22, 26, 29–30, 62–64
Mountague (Montague), Peter, of Boveny, 7
Mountague (Montague), Peter, uncle of Peter Junior, 9
Mountague (Montague), Sarah, 4, 8–10
Mountague (Montague), Thomas, Jr., 8, 10
"Mountain Side," Waugh farm, 36, 38
"Mt. Airy Estate," 34, 41, 46
Mt. Airy Road, 46
Mt. Pisgah Church (Orange Chapel), 38

Municipal Court of Orange County, VA, 19, 22, 24–25, 27–28, 61
Murder ("ordinary"), 12, 16, 62
Murder at Montpelier: Igbo Africans in Virginia (2005), 29

N

Nansemond County, VA (Suffolk, VA), 57
National Society Daughters of the American Revolution (DAR), 36
Native Americans (Indians), 17–18, 34
Negro Run, 14
Negroes (Blacks, African Americans), 12, 15–17, 29
Negrohead Run (Negro-head Run), 14
New York, 59
New York City, 59
Nigeria, Southern, 4
Noden, Hugh, 4, 64

O

Oak Green Farm, 41
Oakwood Cemetery, 43
Ohio River Valley, 19
Ohio Valley region, 19
Old Dominion (Virginia), 18
Orange, VA, County seat, 16, 24, 37, 40
Orange Chapel (Mt. Pisgah Church), 38
Orange County, VA, xi, xiii, 3–4, 8–9, 12, 14–22, 24–25, 30, 34, 36–37, 40, 42, 46, 49, 57, 61–62

Orange County, VA (Population enumeration/distribution, 1782), 17
Orange County Circuit Court, 19, 22, 24–25, 27–28, 61
Orange County Courthouse, First, 13, 22–26, 29, 33, 45, 60–61
Orange County Courthouse, 22, 28
Orange County Historical Society, 15, 32, 47–50
Orange County Militia, 36
Orange County Nursing Home, 42–43
Orange County Order Book 4, (January 23, 1746), 454–455, 31, 45, 50, 61
Orange County Order Books, 45
Orange County Review (1987), 41
Orange County Rescue Squad, 43
Orange Plank Road, 33, 42
"Orange Rangers," 38
Orange Turnpike to Fredericksburg, 37
Overseers, 12, 15
Oyer and Terminer, Court of, xi, 14–15, 25–26, 61–64

P

Pamunkey Neighbors of Orange County, Virginia (1985), 50, 61
Parliament, British, 14, 25
Patriots, 36
Pendleton, James, 62
Pennsylvania, 19–20, 58
Pennsylvania Brigade (Wayne's), 20
Peter (slave), 3, 13–14
"Petit" Treason, Petty, xiii, 11, 13–14, 27–28, 57, 62
Petty Treason ("Petit"), xiii, 11, 13–14, 27–28, 57, 62
Philadelphia, PA, 58

Phillis (slave), 59
Picerno, Nicholas (Nick), 40
Piedmont region, 18–19
Pillory, 23
Pine Stake Road, Orange County, VA, 34, 47
Pine Top, Orange County, VA, 8–9
Poison, 4, 12, 15, 58, 63
Poisoning ("Conjuring"), 4, 12, 15, 29, 58, 63
Pollard, James, 61
Pompey (slave), 12
"Porto Bella," 19
Potter, Harriet, 14
Preddy Funeral Chapel, 43
Prince of Orange (William III), 18
Punishments, English Civil Law, 11–17

Q

Quartermaster Detachment, CSA., 38

R

Raccoon Ford, 20–21, 23, 32, 36–38, 41–43, 45
Raccoon Ford Christian Fellowship, 42, 54
Raccoon Ford Road (Route 611), 20, 34, 46–47, 49, 53
Randolph-Macon College, 42
Randolph-Macon Military Academy, 42
Rapidan (Station), VA, 20, 36–37
Rapidan Line, 21, 35–37, 40
Rapidan River, 18, 20–24, 32–34, 36–37, 42, 46–47
Rappahannock County, VA, 19
Reeves, Matthew, 35

Remembering: A History of Orange County, Virginia (2004), 46, 59
Revolutionary War, 17, 28, 36, 38
Rex v. Eve, xi, 26, 61
Richmond, VA, 58
Richmond-Times Dispatch (1990), 42
Riddle, John, 13
Riddle, Thomas, 13
River Road (Route 636), 20, 43
Riverside Church, 42, 52–54, 56
The Road to Yorktown: Jefferson, Lafayette... (2015), 21
Robinson River, 18
Route 611 (Raccoon Ford Road), 20, 34, 46–47, 49, 53
Route 636 (River Road), 20, 43
Roxbury, Boston, MA, 59
Russell, William, 25–27, 62, 64

S

Secessionist, 40
Schwarz, Philip, 29
Scott, Arthur P., 12–13
Scott, W.W., 14, 30–31
Shenandoah Valley (Valley of Virginia), 19
Sheriff, High (Gentleman), 25–27, 36, 46
Sholl, Peter, 62
The Short Life and Strange Death of Ambrose Madison (2001), 15
"Show trials," 15
Signal stations, Clark Mountain, 21
Simon (slave), 15
Sims, Richard, 15
6th Virginia Cavalry, Co. I, 38
Slaughter, Francis, 61
Slaughter, Robert, 61
Slave poisonings, 15, 29
Slave traders, 4
Slavery, 15–16, 29

Slaves, 15–16, 29
Slaves, lactose intolerance, 29
Slaves of Peter Montague (1718–1745), 3–4, 9–10, 17
Somerville, James, 20
Somerville, Walker, 20
Somerville Ford ("The Governor's Ford), 20, 22–23, 26, 32, 37
Somerville Ford Bridge, 20
"Somervillia," 20
South, The, 22, 40, 58–59
South Carolina, 58
Southwest Mountains (Little Mountains), 21
Sparacio, Ruth, 50, 61
Sparacio, Sam, 50, 61
Spencer, Edward, 25–26, 62
Spotswood, Alexander, 18–20, 22, 33, 46
Spotsylvania County, VA, 4, 8–9, 18–19
Spotsylvania Court House, VA, 9
St. George Parish, Spotsylvania County, VA, 9
St. Mary's Parish, Essex County, VA, 8
St. Paul's Episcopal Church, 43
St. Thomas Parish, Orange County, VA, 8–9, 36
St. Thomas's Episcopal Church, 37
Stevens, John, 10
Stocks (Punishment), 23
Suffolk, VA (Nansemond County), 57
"Summerduck," 36

T

Taylor, Erasmus, 16
Taylor, George, 25–26, 62
Taylor, Thomas, 8
Taylor, Zachary, 61
Tennessee whiskey, 41

Theriott, Ann, 8
Theriott, Elizabeth Ann, 8
Theriott, Peter, 8
Therriatt, Elizabeth, 8
Therriatt, William, 8
Thomas, Joseph, 62
Thomas, Richard, 62
Tinlaw, John, 61
Tobacco, 28
Tom (slave), 16
Traitors, 29
"Traveller" (Robert E. Lee's horse), 37
Treason, xi, 11, 14–25, 57–58, 62
Treason, High, 11–12, 28, 62
Triplett, William, 62
Twice Condemned: Slaves and the Criminal Laws of Virginia, 1705–1865 (1988), 29

U

Union Army, 21
Unionville, VA, 43
U.S. Highway 522 (Zachary Taylor Highway), 20, 24, 38, 43, 47, 56
U.S. Highway 522 Bridge, 20, 24
University of Virginia Hospital, 43

V

Valley of Virginia (Shenandoah Valley), 19
Vietnam, 44
Virginia, State of, 22, 28, 57
Virginia Colony, 7, 18–19, 28, 33, 36, 57, 59
Virginia, Commonwealth of, 22, 28, 57
Virginia frontier, 11–18, 24

Virginia Historical Society, 19, 32, 58
Virginia Magazine of History and Biography (1896), 19, 58
Virginia Militia, 36

W

Walker, Frank S. Jr., 12, 46, 52, 57, 59
Water tower, Mount Airy, 52–55
Waugh, Abner, 36
Waugh, Alec, 51–52
Waugh, Alexander Sr., 30, 36, 46
Waugh, Alexander Jr., 36
Waugh, Charles Alexander, 38
Waugh, Charles Stuart, 30, 38, 40
Waugh, Elizabeth, 36
Waugh Family, 30, 33, 36, 38, 42–44, 46, 48, 51
Waugh Family Cemetery, 40
"Waugh Farm," 34, 47
Waugh farm, "Mountain Side," 36, 38
Waugh farmhouse, Mount Airy, 34, 38, 40, 46, 49, 53–55
Waugh's Ford (Rapidan, VA), 36
Waugh, Gary, 41, 43–44
Waugh, George (Lee?), 36, 38
Waugh, George Lee, 36, 38
Waugh, George Monroe, 42
Waugh, George Morgan, 42
Waugh, John (Parson), 36
Waugh, John (son of Alexander Sr.), 36
Waugh, Lula (Clark), 42
Waugh, Mary, 36
Waugh, Mary Frances (Faulconer), 38
Waugh, Richard, 36
Waugh, Robert Monroe, R. Monroe, xiii, 30, 36, 38, 41–44, 47, 52–53

Waugh, Sarah, 41, 43–44
Waugh, Sarah Battaile, 36
Waugh, Sara Bland Gary, 41, 43
Waugh, Stiles Franklin, 42
Waugh, Wells, 44
Wayne, Anthony ("Mad"), 20–21
Westward expansion, 17, 19
White conspirators, 12, 29
William III of England, Prince of Orange, 18
Williamsburg, VA, 24–25
Winslow, Richard, 25-26, 62
Winter Quarters, Army of Northern Virginia (1863–1864), 36–38, 40
Witches and witchcraft, 29, 34
Women, 27, 29, 57
World War I, 38, 41–42

Y

Yorktown, VA, 20, 38
Young Center for Anabaptist and Pietist Studies (Elizabethtown College), 19, 58

Z

Zachary Taylor Highway (U.S. Highway 522), 20

CPSIA information can be obtained
at www.ICGtesting.com
Printed in the USA
FSOW04n0537210817
37658FS